"THE PREEMINENT CONSUMER ADVOCATE IN THE NUMISMATIC FIELD"* SHARES HIS INVESTMENT KNOW-HOW WITH BOTH THE NOVICE AND THE EXPERT COLLECTOR

Learn:

- How to find and identify rare coins among your pocket change

- How the savvy collector can turn market pressures to his advantage even when dealing with a major player in the coin game

- How to trade coins as commodities, not just curiosities

- How to cash in your profits when the coin market is strong and ride out the storm comfortably when hard times hit

- The economics and psychology of rare coins and precious metals—how to choose coins for fun and profit

ONE-MINUTE COIN EXPERT
The Complete and Easy Guide for Fun and Profit

The New York Times

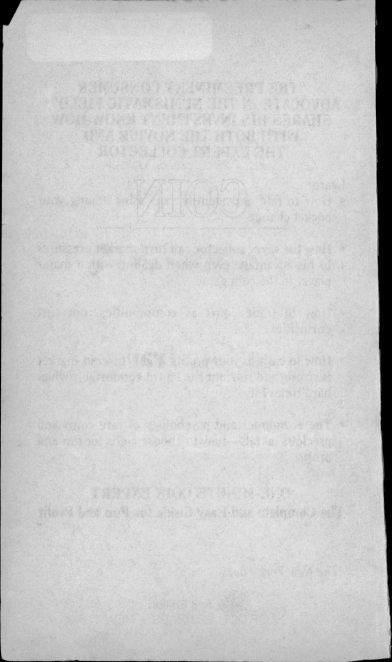

ONE-MINUTE COIN EXPERT

Scott A. Travers

Second Edition
HOUSE OF COLLECTIBLES • NEW YORK

Important Notice. All of the information, including valuations, in this book has been compiled from the most reliable sources, and every effort has been made to eliminate errors and questionable data. Nevertheless, the possibility of error, in a work of such immense scope, always exists. The publisher will not be held responsible for losses that may occur in the purchase, sale, or other transaction of items because of information contained herein. Readers who feel they have discovered errors are invited to *write* and inform us, so they may be corrected in subsequent editions. Those seeking further information on the topics covered in this book are advised to refer to the complete line of *Official Price Guides* published by the House of Collectibles.

Copyright © 1991, 1996 by Scott A. Travers

All rights reserved under International and Pan-American Copyright Conventions.

This is a registered trademark of Random House, Inc.

Published by: House of Collectibles
201 East 50th Street
New York, NY 10022

Distributed by Ballantine Books, a division of Random House, Inc., New York, and simultaneously in Canada by Random House of Canada Limited, Toronto.

Manufactured in the United States of America

http://www.randomhouse.com

ON THE COVER: PhotoProof digital images of 1995 doubled die Lincoln head cent, NGC Mint State 67, valued at $105; and 1897 Barber half dollar, NGC Proof 68, valued at more than $10,000.

Digital images by Allan Willits at NGC

Cover photographs copyright © 1995 by Numismatic Guaranty Corporation

Library of Congress Catalog Card Number: 95-82370

ISBN: 0-676-60027-1

Cover design by Dreu Pennington-McNeil

Second Edition: June 1996

10 9 8 7 6 5 4 3

To my parents

CONTENTS

PREFACE
AND
ACKNOWLEDGMENTS

I especially appreciate the knowledge and advice given to me by so many persons during the preparation of this book. Given the uncertain nature of some of the issues addressed, this book is really a consensus of opinion of many of the contributors consulted. Those contributors are:

John Albanese; Ann Marie Aldrich; Michael Alster; Richard A. Bagg; Dennis Baker; Andrew Barnet; James U. Blanchard, III; Q. David Bowers; Kenneth E. Bressett; Ruthann Brettell; Helen R. Carmody; Jeanne Cavelos; William L. Corsa, Sr.; Beth Deisher; John P. Dessauer; Silvano DiGenova; Al Doyle; William Fivaz; Harry Forman; Leo Frese; Michael Fuljenz; David L. Ganz; Klaus W. Geipel; William T. Gibbs; Richard Giedroyc; Paul M. Green; David Hall; James L. Halperin; David C. Harper; Michael R. Haynes; Leonard H. Hecht; Leon Hendrickson; Charles Hoskins; Steve Ivy; Timothy J. Kochuba; Chester L. Krause; Ronald E. Lasky; Julian Leidman; Robert J. Leuver; Kevin J. Lipton; Tom Mariam; Steve Mayer; Raymond N. Merena; Bob Merrill; James L. Miller; Lee S. Minshull; Richard Nachbar; John Pasciuti, Sr.; Martin Paul; Donn Pearlman; Robert Rachlin; Ed Reiter; Robert S. Riemer; Bernard Rome; Maurice Rosen;

Michael Keith Ruben; Howard Ruff; John Sack; Mark Salzberg; Hugh Sconyers; Howard Segermark; Aaron Shapiro; Michael W. Sherman; John Slack; Harvey Stack; Michael J. Standish; David Sundman; Rick Sundman; Anthony J. Swiatek; James Taylor; Marilyn Van Allen; Armen Vartian; Aimee K. Tihonovich; Leigh H. Weiss; Bob Wilhite; Mark Yaffe; Marc D. Zand, and Keith M. Zaner.

Maurice Rosen was of supreme importance in his assistance in understanding market psychology. John Dessauer's help was invaluable for his expression of ideas regarding coins and precious metals. Marilyn Van Allen and Keith Zaner compiled many of the photographs and coin prices. And Ed Reiter served as my numismatic editor and carefully reviewed and assisted in revising the finished manuscript.

                                         Scott A. Travers

                                         New York
                                         March 1996

INTRODUCTION

Small change can be worth big money.

In the late 1980s, rare coins became the hottest new game in the world of high finance. Promoters pointed to studies showing that coins had outperformed all other major forms of investment, and this attracted thousands of new buyers to the coin market. Since then, the hype has faded and many rare coins have fallen in price. But that actually makes them better values today. And these very good values are within the reach of almost everyone.

At times, the only reach needed is into your pocket or purse. Coins worth hundreds—even thousands—of dollars can be found in otherwise ordinary pocket change. True, it doesn't happen every day. But bettors don't hit the lottery very often either, and that doesn't stop them from playing their numbers religiously week after week. You're much more likely to find a valuable coin in pocket change than you are to win a bundle in the lottery. And the cost—just the face value (or spending value) of the coin—is cheaper by a long shot than what people spend on lottery games.

One-Minute Coin Expert will tell you how to maximize your chances to reap big profits from *your own* small change. It also will provide you with all the tools you need to buy and sell coins effectively, shrewdly—

and profitably—in the bustling coin marketplace, an international network of dealers, collectors, and investors where rare cents are no penny-ante proposition and scarce nickels and dimes are much more than merely a five-and-ten-cent business. By following a series of quick, easy steps, you'll soon be able to transform your coin collection into a healthy bankroll of that other highly popular form of money—the kind you spend!

While certainly important, profit is just one reason why millions of people all around the world collect coins. The hobby is richly rewarding in other ways, as well.

Pick up an old coin and you're literally holding history in your hand. Coins are mirrors of the civilizations that issued them, and they frequently furnish fascinating insights into the life and times of those who made them.

They're more than just mirrors, of course: They're tangible mementos of the cultures in which they were produced; in fact, they're among our most important links with some of mankind's greatest, most glorious eras. The temples of ancient Athens have vanished or lie in ruins, but many lovely coins endure as tangible reminders of the grandeur that was Greece.

1804 coin front or "obverse" from a quarter dollar sold for a low six-figure price. An 1804 silver dollar with this obverse design sold for $990,000 in 1989. (Photo courtesy Andrew Barnet)

Coins are also tiny works of art. Although they may be only millimeters wide, many are exquisitely beautiful and their owners take great pride in possessing and displaying them.

Collectors enjoy assembling sets of coins. Finding a coin you need—whether in pocket change, a piggy bank, or even a dealer's display case—is a source of satisfaction and even exhilaration. It's just like digging up buried treasure.

Coin collecting didn't come into its own as a pastime for the masses until relatively recently. At one time, it was known as "The Hobby of Kings" because only noblemen had the time and money to indulge in it. During the last few decades, interest and involvement in this stimulating pastime have multiplied geometrically, and "The Hobby of Kings" has now become "The King of Hobbies" instead.

The coin market, too, has undergone major changes in recent years. A generation ago, it was populated almost exclusively by mom-and-pop dealers and small collectors. But now, well-heeled investors have joined the hunt, altering the ground rules fundamentally and raising the stakes—and many of the prices—enormously.

Coin collecting still holds great appeal for small collectors; it's avidly pursued by multitudes of people— including several million Americans—in virtually every age group and income bracket. This widespread demand provides a solid base for the coin market, serving as an important underpinning for the price structure. Today, however, rare coins are no longer mere collectibles. In a word, they have become an *investment*—an investment whose returns can be spectacular.

Investors' interest in coins peaked in the late 1980s,

when several Wall Street firms became active, aggressive participants in the coin market. Unfortunately, that involvement proved to be premature. Coin prices soared initially amid the euphoria generated by these new "players," but after the frenzy subsided, price levels also fell back. Far from being a source of concern, this represents a wonderful opportunity: The lower prices make the market even more attractive for potential investors today.

The coin market has grown not only in size but also in sophistication. For example, a 70-point grading system is now used to denote coins' "condition," or state of preservation. The number 70 refers to a coin which is perfect—which has no nicks or scratches and never has been passed from hand to hand. As a coin goes from hand to hand, the metal wears down and that coin loses detail which can never be recovered. Coins that have lost this detail are said to be "circulated."

The market's greater complexity is evident, as well, from the way coins are now bought and sold. Dealers conduct transactions on computerized trading networks; and neighborhood coin shops, while far from extinct, are dwarfed today by large, high-profile dealerships with international clienteles and multimillion-dollar inventories and sales. In other ways, however, buying and selling coins is really simpler—for those who know what they're doing and where they're going.

Some people have trouble telling the difference between coins which have no scratches, and have not been spent, and other coins which have passed through many hands and been worn down. "Certification" services give people an impartial opinion as to how worn—or how new—a coin is. These organizations seal each coin in a special plastic holder designed so the coin cannot be easily removed. A paper insert stating the service's grading is sealed inside this holder with the coin. Any attempt to remove the coin or insert, or to change the grading on the insert, can be easily detected.

Independent grading services have removed much of the guesswork—and much of the risk—from buying and selling coins. A number of certified coins are so widely accepted, in fact, that many dealers feel comfortable making offers for them on a sight-unseen basis. Although most buyers now prefer to look at coins first, and purchase them on a sight-seen basis, the sight-unseen concept has made it possible for even neophytes to participate successfully in the coin market.

The ability to grade coins accurately is partly a science, partly an art. *You* don't need to be an expert grader; the grading services' expertise provides you with a fine security blanket. Still, you should equip yourself with a fundamental knowledge of what's involved—and once understood, the elements are simple.

One-Minute Coin Expert makes them even simpler by showing you an easy, enjoyable way to determine the grade of a coin by reviewing its key components.

Like any investment field, the rare coin market goes up and down. And how you "play the game" goes a long way toward determining how much money you make. *One-Minute Coin Expert* gives you a big head start and an inside track. Knowledge is the key. Many current players lack the knowledge they need to be successful— but after reading this book, you'll be ready to compete like a seasoned veteran.

One-Minute Coin Expert will tell you what to look for. Whether you're simply a casual accumulator—someone who pulls odd-looking coins out of pocket change and sticks them away in a drawer—or a high-powered investor who buys expensive coins for thousands of dollars apiece, this book will give you all the information you need to maximize your return on the time and money you spend.

I'll tell you how to cash in your profits when the coin market is strong. And I'll also explain how to ride out the storm comfortably when hard times hit.

One-Minute Coin Expert provides you with a maximum of information in a minimum of time. I'll give you a simple, straightforward blueprint of how the market works and how it can be made to work for you, enabling you to turn your small change into big money.

I'll start by explaining why people save coins, and examine the four different categories into which most of these people fall. Then I'll tell you more about coins in general, including how to spot the mint marks on U.S. coins—small symbols that can add enormous value.

In Chapter Two, I'll give you a checklist of valuable coins that can and do appear in ordinary pocket change. Then, in Chapter Three, I'll tell you about still other worthwhile coins that won't be in your pocket change but may very well turn up around your home—perhaps in a cigar box or dresser drawer.

Once you know which dates and mint marks to look for, I'll take you on a guided tour of the coin market, showing you what makes it tick and how you can get the edge on everyone else when buying or selling coins. I'll make you an instant expert not only on grading coins but also on trading them. And I'll tell you how to spot the coins with the greatest potential—the ones that are likely to go up in value faster and farther than all the rest. I'll even give you a secret list of my personal Top Ten recommendations.

Coins and precious metals are closely interrelated. I'll show you just how they work together, and how this can provide you with golden opportunities to pocket sizable profits.

Before we're through, I'll also take you behind the scenes in a captivating real-life drama featuring drug dealers, coin dealers, and the U.S. government.

As this book is written, the coin market is in a protracted slump and many prices are well below the levels they enjoyed at the market's last big peak in mid-1989. Many analysts see this as a great opportunity. In traditional investment areas such as stocks, long bear markets frequently are followed by especially dramatic bull-market upturns. Although there is no guarantee that the coin market will come back to the price levels of the past, you're sure to be a winner if you follow the recommendations in this book. You may not always reap huge profits from the coins you find and buy, but you'll have a life-long sense of appreciation for the beauty, romance, and history they possess.

One-Minute Coin Expert is meant to do just what the title suggests: make you an expert.

You'll learn how to spot bargains . . . how to pick coins that will rise in value quickly . . . how to grade coins . . . how to buy and sell . . . how to understand market psychology . . . how to protect your investments from the tax man. In short, you'll learn how to play this intriguing, potentially lucrative money game—and how to win!

CHAPTER 1

YOU CAN BE AN EXPERT

This is a book on how to become an expert on coins.

Expertise on coins can take many forms. It can mean becoming adroit at checking pocket change for coins that will bring you a financial windfall. It also can mean becoming astute at spending money on coins, whether you're reaching into your pocket for one hundred dollars to buy a rare coin, or even reaching deep into your bank account for many thousands of dollars to spend on extremely rare coins in hopes of achieving a profit.

Whatever your degree of involvement, this book will make you an expert. And if you become an expert, you can profit from rare coins at every level of involvement, regardless of whether current market conditions are good or bad.

At one time or another, possibly without even realizing it, just about everyone thinks about coins as an investment. It happens, for example, when a really old coin turns up in your change or in your travels, or when you get a coin that just doesn't look right—one, for example, on which the date and some of the words are misprinted.

Many of us have had this experience. And when it happens, we invariably want to know two things: What's it worth, and will I make more money if I sell it now or later?

You don't have to wait for scarce and valuable coins to come along; you can go looking for them. And you can make money by buying and selling scarce coins. Many such coins today are authenticated and graded by independent experts and then encased in special plastic holders. This process assures the buyer that the grade, or level of preservation, is being properly stated by the seller. "Certified" coins change hands readily on nationwide trading networks and greatly enhance the appeal of rare coins to traditional investors.

I've come up with simple, easy-to-follow guidelines that will take you step by step through the process of identifying good values at all levels of the coin-buying spectrum. Follow these steps and you'll not only know what to look for, but also what to do with the coins once you have them.

Coins go up and down in value frequently; the coin market has peaks and valleys. But I'll show you how to make money in all kinds of markets—when coins are red-hot and also when prices are in a tailspin. That, after all, is the sign of a real expert: knowing how to thrive whether the coin market is rallying or is in one of its characteristic cyclical downturns.

WHY PEOPLE ACQUIRE COINS

People save coins for a number of different reasons. Some find them appealing as miniature works of art. Others are intrigued by the rich historical significance they possess. Many simply enjoy the challenge of pursuing something rare, elusive, and valuable. And, not least of all, many are attracted by the marvelous track record rare coins have achieved as good investments. Obviously, a great many people collect rare coins for *all* these different reasons, to a greater or lesser degree.

Finding something valuable is understandably thrilling, and many scarce coins do turn up in ordinary pocket change. I'll furnish a list of such coins in Chapter Two. Realistically, though, many rare coins have to be purchased.

Billions of dollars are spent on rare coins every year, and United States coins are by far the biggest segment of that market. In large part, that's because Americans account for the single biggest group of collectors in the world, as well as being among the most affluent. But other factors also have a bearing. For one thing, U.S. coins require less in-depth knowledge than ancient coins or international coins from the modern era. For another thing, the U.S. coin market is an easy-entry, easy-exit field with no regulation by the government—and many entrepreneurs find this appealing.

THE COIN BUYER SPECTRUM

The rare coin market is really a spectrum of different kinds of buyers. While one group of buyers may have different motivations from other groups, all are integral parts of the overall market—and all, in a real sense, are interdependent.

We can better understand who buys and saves coins, and why, by looking at the following graphic:

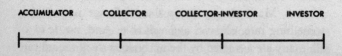

ACCUMULATOR   COLLECTOR   COLLECTOR-INVESTOR   INVESTOR

Accumulators   Accumulators are people who save coins haphazardly, without a particular pattern or plan of action. Many are undoubtedly attracted by the same positive qualities that motivate collectors and investors: the physical appeal of the coins and the notion of selling them for a profit, for example. But these objectives are only vaguely defined.

An accumulator may have sugar bowls or jars filled with coins, but they're probably not arranged in any special order and he probably doesn't have a very good idea what they're worth—even though some of them may be worth a great deal.

Collectors   In theory, a collector is someone who purchases coins with no regard at all for their profit potential—someone who is motivated strictly by such factors as aesthetics and historical significance. If a collector purchased a coin for $100 and its value went up to $1,000, he wouldn't even consider selling that coin, since he wouldn't have any interest in the coin's financial aspects. Theoretically, a collector also wouldn't concern himself with how much he had to pay to obtain a coin.

Collectors enjoy assembling coins in sets, and they strive for completeness in those sets. Lincoln cents with wheat stalks on the reverse were issued, for example, from 1909 to 1958. A collector would be interested in putting together representative Lincoln cents from each of those years so that she would have a complete set. Some collectors also like to assemble "type" collections, consisting of one coin from each of a number of different series. A twentieth-century type set of U.S. coins, for instance, would include one example of every different U.S. coin issued since 1901. A "type" coin is a representative example of a major coin variety but not a rare date of that variety.

Investors   On the other end of the spectrum, at the right-hand side of our graphic, is the investor. Unlike the collector, the investor pays close attention to inflation, interest rates, the size of the money supply—and, in short, the economic justification for purchasing rare coins. The quintessential investor, in fact, would be concerned *only* with profit, and not at all with coins' aesthetics and history.

Collector/Investors   In practical terms, no one is ever a totally solid collector or solid investor. Even the most dedicated collectors can't be completely oblivious to the cost and the value of their coins. And even the most profit-oriented investor can't completely ignore the intangible allure of beautiful coins.

The collector/investor combines the best of both worlds. This is a person who buys coins not only for their cultural, historical, and artistic appeal, but also to make a profit. The collector/investor represents a new breed of coin buyer, and a very healthy one.

OLD-TIME COLLECTING

Years ago, many people set aside interesting coins: circulated coins they found in pocket change, rolls of brand new coins they obtained at face value from the bank, or possibly government proof sets they purchased for modest premiums from the Mint. These coins may not have been particularly valuable at the time, but over the years coin collecting has evolved from a small hobby into a big business. And today, these tiny treasures may very well command enormous premiums.

As with anything else, it's a matter of supply and demand. Many of these coins, rolls, and proof sets have been in small supply since the day they were made. But years ago, the number of collectors was also relatively small, so demand for these coins remained at moderate levels. That served to hold down their prices.

Coin collecting became much more popular in the early 1960s. Thousands and thousands of newcomers started looking for low-mintage coins in their pocket change; many would go the bank and get rolls of coins every week, then take them home and pick out the scarcer pieces. During that period, many people also began to purchase proof sets from the government every year. The expansion continued and accelerated during the 1970s and into the 1980s.

THE COMING OF THE INVESTOR

Investors began to enter the coin market in large numbers in the mid to late 1970s. The timing was no accident: Coins, like precious metals, have come to be viewed as hedges against economic calamities, and the late 1970s were years of unusual turbulence economically. Inflation was on the rise and many people were skeptical of the government's ability to control it. They also were wary of conventional investments such as stocks.

Driven by these fears, many turned to tangible assets and diverted large sums of money into gold, silver, and other such investments—including coins. Some combined their interest in coins and precious metals by buying *bullion coins.* These are coins whose value goes up or down in accordance with the value of the metal they contain—usually gold or silver. We'll discuss these in greater detail in a later chapter.

During the period ending in early 1980, the coin market experienced the most tremendous boom it has ever enjoyed.

THE GROWTH OF COLLECTING/INVESTING

As the number of collectors and investors expanded, so did the demand for better-date coins. The results were entirely predictable: As market demand increased for a fixed (and small) supply, prices began to escalate dramatically. At the same time, more and more people began to approach rare coins as both a collecting outlet and an investment.

Many collector/investors are baby boomers grown up: people who possibly started collecting coins when they were twelve or thirteen years old and built a solid foundation, then took a hiatus to pursue other interests such as college, courtship, and careers. Many of these collector/investors returned to the field in the mid to late 1980s and returned with a vengeance, bringing with them not only their strong foundation in coins but also finely honed minds and high incomes—testaments to their high degree of success at institutions of higher learning and in their careers.

These people are buying coins like there's no tomorrow. They have substantial sums of money at their disposal and they're savoring the chance to spend it on desirable coins. They appreciate every aspect of coins, including the one which can benefit *your* pocketbook: the financial aspect.

Collector/investors have added to the market's volatile nature—its susceptibility to going up or down in value very quickly.

Collectors and investors—and collector/investors— come in different degrees. Many, for example, would fall between the *Collector* and *Collector/Investor* locations on our graphic. The coin buyer spectrum is broad, diverse, and continuous, and buyers can be found across that spectrum.

THREE KINDS OF RARE COINS

For the purposes of this book, there are basically three different kinds of valuable coins.

One group consists of coins it's possible to come across in pocket change. These coins are described in Chapter Two.

Another group consists of coins you'd have to purchase. These tend to be coins with very low mintages and in very high grades or levels of preservation. They're the kind of coins investors favor. We'll look at these in greater detail in later chapters.

The third group of coins consists of what might be called "cigar-box rarities." They're coins that you might find in a cigar box up in the attic, or stashed away in a shoe box on a shelf at the back of a closet.

"Cigar-box rarities" probably wouldn't be found in pocket change. Many are coins that aren't being minted anymore. But most people have such coins sitting around the house, or know of a friend or relative who does. Often, they've been handed down by relatives who found them— or maybe even purchased them—years ago. If so, they may be quite valuable. Many coins that were looked upon as common fifty years ago, or even twenty-five years ago, are worth large sums of money in the current marketplace.

The cigar-box rarities which are most valuable—and which you might have a chance of finding—are listed in Chapter Three, along with their fair market value.

There's an excellent chance that some of these scarce coins—coins that have become quite valuable over the years—may be sitting in *your* attic, or perhaps in a jewelry case in the back of a dresser drawer. Perhaps your father put them there many years ago, when they were still regarded as not of great consequence, then forgot them. Or maybe they've been handed down through generations that go back even farther.

PROOF SETS AND MINT SETS

A proof set is a group of specimen-quality coins, usually bearing a uniform date and housed in protective packaging. Proof coins are made by taking special, highly polished coin blanks and striking them several times with highly polished dies. These are considered the highest-quality coins available. The United States Mint offers proof sets for sale to the public every year.

A mint set, by contrast, consists of business-strike coins: the kind that are produced for circulation. A mint set contains one example of each different coin struck for circulation in any given year by each of the different mints. The coins in such a set may have been chosen carefully, but they're business strikes just the same.

Normally, a proof set costs more than a mint set when purchased from the government and also has higher value in the resale market. However, on occasion a mint set may be more valuable in the resale market than the corresponding proof set for that year. This may happen, for example, if the mint set contains a coin that wasn't actually made for general use. Since the mint set then contains the only circulation-quality example, that coin and that set will command an added premium.

MINT MARKS AND HOW TO LOCATE THEM

Many coins' values are enhanced by the presence of *mint marks*. These are little letters denoting the mint facility where the coins were manufactured.

During its earliest years, the United States Mint had only one production plant—in Philadelphia—and so there was no need to identify the source of any coins. As the nation grew and coinage requirements rose, branch mints were established in cities around the country. Each of these branches placed a mint mark on its coins to distinguish them readily from those being made at other mints.

Following are the letters used on U.S. coins to denote branch mints:

C—Charlotte, North Carolina (1838–1861, gold coins only)
CC—Carson City, Nevada (1870–1893)
D—Dahlonega, Georgia (1838–1861, gold coins only)
D—Denver (1906 to date)
O—New Orleans (1838–1909)
S—San Francisco (1854 to date)
W—West Point, New York (1984 to date)

* * *

Throughout most of U.S. history, coins produced at the main mint in Philadelphia carried no mint mark. Their origin was denoted by the *absence* of any such mark. In recent years, however, a small P has been placed on most coins produced in Philadelphia. This practice began in 1979, when the P mint mark was used on the Susan B. Anthony dollar. The following year, it was added to all other coins with one exception: No P has been used on Lincoln cents.

A Philadelphia mint mark was used one other time. During World War II, nickel was urgently needed for war-related purposes, so from 1942 through 1945 the Mint used a substitute alloy without any nickel in making five-cent pieces. The emergency alloy's components were copper, silver, and manganese. To denote this change in composition, the Mint placed large mint marks above Monticello's dome on the coins' reverse—including a large, slender P on non-nickel "nickels" produced during those years in Philadelphia. (The reverse of a coin is what is commonly known as the "tails" side and carries the monetary value of the coin. The obverse or "heads" side commonly carries a portrait and the year of the coin's issue.)

On nineteenth-century coins, the mint mark was usually placed at the base of the reverse, below the wreath or eagle depicted on that side. Mint marks' locations have varied a great deal more on twentieth-century coins, and some coins have carried them in several different places at different times.

Here's a checklist of where to look for mint marks on some of the coins you're most likely to encounter in current pocket change or older hoards:

- Lincoln cent (1909 to date)—below the date.
- Indian Head cent (1859–1909)—below the wreath

(mint marks appear only on coins dated 1908 and 1909).

- Jefferson nickel (1938 to date)—on the reverse, to the right of Monticello, on most dates from 1938 to 1964; above Monticello on war nickels from 1942 to 1945; below the date from 1968 to the present.
- Buffalo nickel (1913–1938)—on the reverse, below the words *FIVE CENTS*.
- Liberty Head nickel (1883–1912)—on the reverse, to the left of the word *CENTS* (mint marks appear only on coins dated 1912).
- Roosevelt dime (1946 to date)—on the reverse, to the left of the torch's base, from 1946 to 1964; above the date from 1968 to the present.
- "Mercury" dime (1916–1945)—on the reverse, to the left of the fasces (the symbolic bundle of rods).
- Barber dime (1892–1916)—below the wreath.
- Washington quarter (1932 to date)—below the wreath from 1932 to 1964; to the right of George Washington's pigtail from 1968 to the present.
- Standing Liberty quarter (1916–1930)—to the left of the date. (*NOTE:* The M to the right of the date is not a mint mark; it stands for Hermon MacNeil, the coin's designer.)
- Barber quarter (1892–1916)—below the eagle.
- Kennedy half dollar (1964 to date)—to the left of the eagle's tail feathers in 1964; below John F. Kennedy's neck from 1968 to the present.
- Walking Liberty half dollar (1916–1947)—on the front, below *IN GOD WE TRUST*, in 1916 and 1917; on the reverse, above and to the left of *HALF DOLLAR*, from 1917 to 1947 (1917 examples come in both varieties).

- Barber half dollar (1892–1915)—below the eagle.
- Anthony dollar (1979–1981)—above Susan B. Anthony's right shoulder.
- Eisenhower dollar (1971–1978)—below Dwight D. Eisenhower's neck.
- Peace silver dollar (1921–1935)—on the reverse, below the word *ONE*.
- Morgan silver dollar (1878–1921)—below the wreath.
- Saint-Gaudens $20 gold piece (1907–1933)—above the date.
- Liberty Head $20 gold piece (1850–1907)—below the eagle.

Now that you have some idea of where you fall on the collector/investor spectrum and the different types of coins that are available to you, it's time to take a closer look at the coins you already have—in your pocket change.

CHAPTER 2

A FORTUNE IN
POCKET CHANGE

A penny saved isn't always a penny earned. It can be *thousands* or *millions* of pennies earned if the penny in question is rare.

A client of mine discovered this recently when he looked through a box of old coins in the attic of his grandmother's home. Included in that hoard were several Lincoln cents dated 1909. They turned out to be extremely scarce coins worth hundreds of dollars apiece—yet they had been pulled out of pocket change many years before. Thus, the initial "investment" had been just a penny apiece.

That wasn't *all* my client found. Altogether, that box of coins probably contained only a few hundred dollars in face value—but because some of the coins were rare and especially well preserved, the tiny keepsakes were worth more than *a quarter of a million dollars* as collector's items. And they hadn't cost a penny more than "face" when the grandmother and other family members set them aside.

This experience is hardly an isolated case. Over the years, untold thousands of people have come across valuable coins in their pockets or purses, or set aside coins for sentimental reasons and learned later to their amazement that those coins had soared in value as collectibles.

MISSTRIKES AND MINT MARKS

Sometimes the value of such coins stems from the fact that they are "misstrikes": coins with obvious errors that somehow eluded detection at the mint where they were made. Other times, they're valuable because they display an important identifying mark, such as a mint mark. As I explained in Chapter One, coins produced at certain mints are stamped with little letters denoting the place of manufacture. Coins made at the Denver Mint have a small letter D, while those produced at the San Francisco Mint have an S.

Worth $35. *1970 Roosevelt dime struck off-center and too many times at the Denver Mint. (Photo courtesy* Coin World*)*

The presence—or absence—of a mint mark can sometimes make a difference of hundreds or thousands of dollars in the value of certain coins. Those 1909 Lincoln cents found by my client, for instance, had a small letter S under the date. That means they were made at the San Francisco Mint. They also had the letters V.D.B. at the base of the reverse, or "tails" side. These are the initials of Victor D. Brenner, the artist who designed the Lincoln cent. Without the S mint mark and the initials of the designer, those pennies would be worth just two or three dollars apiece. Those letters were missing on most of the Lincoln cents produced in 1909. Only a few displayed them—and with coins as with anything else, value is determined by supply and demand. The supply of these coins is small, the demand is great, and therefore the value is high.

Worth $300. *1909-S V.D.B. Lincoln cent received in change at a supermarket. (Photo courtesy* Coin World*)*

Most of these 1909-S V.D.B. cents were put away years ago by collectors. But some turn up in ordinary pocket change even now. Not long ago, a hospital employee in Los Angeles got an unusual cent in change at a local supermarket. She showed it to a friend at the hospital, seventy-nine-year-old Sid Lindenbaum, who worked there as a volunteer. Lindenbaum, a longtime coin collector, looked at the strange cent under a magnifying glass—and sure enough, it had both the S and the V.D.B.

"Miracles can still happen!" Lindenbaum exclaimed in an interview with a newspaper reporter. "I've been collecting coins for over sixty years and this is a first."

The coin had some wear, but wasn't in bad condition considering its age—two years older than Lindenbaum himself. Buying one would have cost the veteran hobbyist a couple of hundred dollars. Doing the right thing, he compensated his friend and both shared the joy of the occasion.

"I paid her more than she ever dreamt a Lincoln penny could possibly be worth, and she was as deliriously happy as I was," Lindenbaum told the reporter.

Some coins are valuable because they *lack* a mint mark. A case in point occurred in 1982, when the Philadelphia

Mint made a small number of dimes without the mint mark P which normally appears just above the date on coins from that mint. Because of that omission and the scarcity of these dimes, collectors soon began to bid up the price. If one of these coins shows up in your change next time you go to the store, put it in a safe place: It's worth at least $50—and possibly several times more, depending on what condition it's in.

PROFITABLE MISTAKES

"Mint errors"—oddball coins—make great conversation pieces, and finding one can sometimes be the next best thing to digging up buried treasure.

Consider these examples:

- In 1955, odd-looking cents began appearing in upstate New York and New England. The date and lettering on the "heads" side of these coins (the side called the "obverse" by collectors) had a double image—a sort of shadow effect. Thousands of these pennies popped up in people's change.

Worth $385. *1955 doubled-die Lincoln cent, a mint error. This example is circulated or worn. (Photo courtesy* Coin World).

At that time, cigarettes cost eighteen cents a pack and people who bought them in vending machines would insert twenty cents and get their two cents change tucked inside the cellophane in the pack. On occasion, both these coins would be double-image cents. Lots of people saved them as curiosities—and today they're glad they did: These 1955 "doubled-die" cents, as collectors call them, are now worth almost $400 even in used condition. Brand new, they're worth well over $1,000 apiece.

- In 1972, similar double-image cents began turning up in the East, especially in and around Philadelphia. These weren't quite as obvious as the ones from 1955, and they seemed to be somewhat more numerous. Nonetheless, they were soon bringing premiums of well over $100 apiece. Some show up in pocket change even now—and when they do, they're readily salable to dealers and collectors for $50 to $200, depending on how well preserved they are.

Worth $225. *1972 doubled-die Lincoln cent, a mint error. This example is new and has not been spent. Notice the prominent doubling of the letters, as the close-up indicates. (Photo courtesy* Coin World)

Worth $40. *1995 doubled-die Lincoln cent, a mint error.*
Doubling is most visible on LIBERTY, shown here blown up.
(Photo courtesy Coin World*)*

- In 1995, thousands of Lincoln cents minted in Philadelphia (without a mint mark) turned up with doubling on the obverse. The error is most obvious in the word LIBERTY. These coins were being sold for $40 or so by the end of the year. Values highest in top mint condition.
- In 1937, an especially fascinating error was discovered on certain Buffalo nickels. For those of you too young to remember them, let me explain that these well-loved coins had the portrait of an Indian on the "heads" side and a realistic likeness of a bison on the reverse.

Worth $150. *1937 Buffalo nickel struck by the Denver Mint. The weakness of the right leg (left to you) has led to collectors calling this the "three-legged Buffalo." (Photo courtesy* Coin World)

On a small number of 1937 nickels made at the Denver Mint, the bison's right front leg appeared to be missing. These "three-legged" nickels became extremely popular with collectors, and remain in great demand to this day. You won't find Buffalo nickels in pocket change today, but chances are good that you—or a member of your family—may have a few stuck away in a dresser or desk. If so, check the dates and if you find any dated 1937, count the legs on the bison. A three-legged nickel can be worth many hundreds of dollars in top condition.

LOW-MINTAGE COINS

In 1950, the government made only about two million Jefferson nickels at the branch mint in Denver. That's far below normal production levels. Each of these Denver nickels carried a small letter D just to the right of the building on the back of the coin (Monticello, the home of Thomas Jefferson). Collectors got wind that the nickels were scarce and rushed to their banks. They saved so many that hardly any entered circulation. Within a few years, these nickels were selling for $30 apiece. Some can still be found in circulation, and even in worn condition they're worth about $5 each.

Sometimes people put away coins from special years—years that have personal meaning to them, or years when new coins first appear. Many people saved Kennedy half dollars when those were first produced in 1964.

I know of one woman born in 1921 whose parents assembled a set of all the U.S. coins bearing that date. They did this soon after their child's birth, putting together the set from coins they obtained at their local bank—coins that had never been spent and were still mint fresh. Twenty-one years later, on their daughter's wedding day, they gave her the coins. As luck would have it, the mintage levels of most U.S. coins were unusually low during 1921. As a result, the coins in this set are extremely desirable to dealers and collectors. In fact, this meticulously preserved set—formed by noncollectors for a total of just a few dollars—is now worth more than $50,000. This felicitous set of coins, a birth memento that later became a wedding gift, is now a valued nest egg, helping to secure the woman's golden years.

PROOF SETS

Birth-year tributes are much more common now than they were back in 1921. But rather than obtaining ordinary coins from a bank, parents today frequently purchase current-year "proofsets" from the government or a coin shop.

The United States Mint makes two or three million proof sets every year. Each set contains special, high-quality examples of all the current coins—one example each of the cent, nickel, dime, quarter, and half dollar. These coins are produced by a painstaking process which gives them shimmering mirrorlike surfaces and a frosty appearance on the high points. Each set is housed in a plastic presentation case suitable for display. At present, the cost of these sets is $12.50 apiece.

Proof sets, too, contain mint errors now and then. And, when they do, the coins in question can be worth a lot of money.

As in the case of regular coins, the error often takes the form of a missing mint mark. That happened, for instance, in 1970, when someone forgot to stamp the letter S above the date on a small number of dimes produced for that year's proof sets. All the proof coins were made at the branch mint in San Francisco and should have carried the mint mark—but an estimated 2,200 dimes did not. Today, those dimes are worth $700 apiece.

A similar error occurred with nickels in 1971. In an estimated 1,655 proof sets that year, the Jefferson nickel was missing the S mint mark. Today, each one is worth close to $1,000.

Worth $700. *1971 no-S proof Jefferson nickel. All of the proof coins were struck in San Francisco and were supposed to have carried the S mint mark. (Photo courtesy* Coin World)

History has a way of repeating itself at Uncle Sam's mints. In 1983, the S turned up missing again on the dimes in a small number of proof sets. These mint errors are now bringing $200 to $300 apiece. And in 1990, the S was missing on Lincoln cents in 3,555 proof sets. One collector in Washington State bought four 1990 proof sets from the Mint and all four contained no-S cents. He sold the sets to a dealer for $1,400 apiece, or a total of $5,600—a very tidy return on his $44 investment.

Worth $1,500. *1990 no-S proof Lincoln cent. Again, someone at the mint left off the S. It should have appeared just under the date. (Photo courtesy Krause Publications)*

One of the most desirable of these mint-error proof coins is the no-S proof dime of 1968. It's thought that fewer than five hundred examples of this coin were produced, and each has a market value of $6,000 to $7,000 at this writing.

Obviously, your chances of finding a $6,000 coin in pocket change, or in a low-cost proof set, are remote. But they're no more remote than your chances of scoring a $6,000 win in a lottery. And I'd be willing to bet you'll spend a lot less money—and have a lot more fun—seeking your fortune in pennies, nickels, and dimes than in random numbers.

A 1989 RARITY

Finding a rare coin in a proof set isn't quite the same as finding one in pocket change. You do have to spend a modest premium above the face value to get the proof set. But the thrill of discovery, the sense of satisfaction, and the joy of ownership are really no different at all. And the profits are equally real and equally high.

Proof sets aren't the only special coins sold to the public by the government. In recent years, the U.S. Mint has also made a number of "commemorative" coins—coins produced in honor of noteworthy people or events. In 1986, for example, the Mint made three coins for the one hundredth anniversary of the Statue of Liberty. And in 1987, it produced two special coins as a two hundredth-birthday tribute to the nation's Constitution.

In 1989, the Mint produced three special coins to honor the U.S. Congress on its two hundredth anniversary. One of these, a silver dollar, was sold to collectors and other interested purchasers for $23 each. A few of the Congress silver dollars were found to have a seldom-seen error—and as this is written, coins with this error are being bought and sold for prices in excess of $600 apiece.

The error involves a feature known as the "rotation" of the coin. On most U.S. coins, the "heads" and "tails" designs are engraved in diametrically opposite positions; when the obverse design is right side up, the reverse design is upside down. To see what I mean, take a quarter out of your pocket and hold it in your hand. Position it so that George Washington's portrait is right side up, with the date at the bottom. Flip the coin over, from north to south, and the eagle should be standing straight up. (If it isn't, you've got an error coin that may be worth a premium to collectors.)

On a small number of 1989 Congress silver dollars, the reverse is rotated 180 degrees from this normal position. If you flip one of *these* coins in the manner I just described, from north to south, it will look upside down.

This may not seem like much of an error to you, but many collectors view it as a great rarity and they're willing to pay a correspondingly great premium. Coin dealer Anthony Swiatek of Manhasset, New York, the world's preeminent authority on U.S. commemorative coinage, believes there are only about two hundred of these coins in existence and recently told me that, in his opinion, these coins could rise in value to $1,000 apiece. And he predicts their trading range won't fall below $700. All this for a coin many people purchased in 1989 for $23!

THE 1943 "COPPER" CENT

One of the most famous of all United States coins is the 1943 bronze Lincoln cent—widely and inaccurately referred to by many laypersons as the 1943 "copper" cent. (The actual coinage metal, bronze, is an alloy of copper, tin, and zinc.) Millions of noncollectors—people who don't know the first thing about coin collecting—have heard about this coin, know it's worth a great deal of money, and have made at least a cursory attempt to locate one in their pocket change.

Worth $15,000 each. *1943 bronze Lincoln cent (right) should have been struck in steel. 1944-D steel Lincoln cent (left) should have been struck in bronze. (Photos courtesy Tom Mulvaney and Coin World)*

By 1943, World War II was at a crucial stage and the war effort permeated every aspect of American society. Coinage was no exception. Copper was urgently needed for battlefield uses, and to help conserve the supply of this critical metal the United States Mint suspended production of bronze ("copper") cents and made the coins instead from steel with a coating of zinc. These "white" cents proved unsuitable almost at once; for one thing, people confused them with the dime. As a result, they were minted for just that one year.

Official government records make no mention of regular bronze cents dated 1943; as far as the Mint was concerned, it never made any. However, it's well established that a few such coins—probably fewer than fifty—do exist. Apparently, a few bronze coin blanks were still in a hopper at the end of production in 1942 and somehow got stamped along with the new steel cents in 1943.

For many years, a story made the rounds that the Ford Motor Company would give a new car to anyone finding a 1943 "copper" cent. That story was unfounded, but anyone fortunate enough to find such a coin today could certainly parlay it into a new car, Ford or otherwise. A few years ago, one of these cents changed hands for $10,000.

A word of caution: Over the years, con artists have copper-plated a number of steel 1943 cents and tried to pass them off as rare bronze cents of that date. These can be detected quite easily with a magnet: Being made of steel, they'll be attracted to the magnet, while genuine bronze cents will not be.

CHECK THAT CHANGE!

Your chances of finding a 1943 copper cent or a 1909-S V.D.B. cent in pocket change are diminished by the fact that in 1959 the Lincoln cent's reverse got a new design. Since that time, the back of the coin has portrayed the Lincoln Memorial. With the passage of time, the earlier Lincoln cents—with two sheaves of wheat displayed on the reverse—have grown steadily harder to find in circulation. As a result, these "wheat-ears" cents are conspicuous when they do appear in change and therefore are quickly set aside. Likewise, a Buffalo nickel (three-legged or otherwise) would stand out from other coins if it showed up in circulation, and that reduces your chances of finding one of these.

There are many scarce and valuable coins waiting for lucky finders in cash drawers, sugar bowls, pockets, and purses today—but, for the most part, these are coins that blend in with the rest of our current coinage. Their basic design is the same, they're made of the same metal, and at first glance they don't look any different.

While they may *look* ordinary, these coins can often be like nuggets of high-grade gold for the prospectors lucky enough to find them.

To give you an idea of the quantity and diversity of these coins, I've compiled a list including some typical illustrations. I've limited this list to coins whose common counterparts are still routinely seen in circulation. It doesn't contain Buffalo nickels or pre-1959 Lincoln cents, for example, since those are seldom encountered anymore and any that did turn up—even common ones—would be set aside almost at once as curiosities. That, of course, would minimize the chances for finding pocket-change rarities of those types.

To readily identify some of the following coins, you may need a magnifying glass. But an inexpensive glass with 5-power magnification will do just fine.

Keep in mind that if you find one of these coins and offer it for sale to a dealer, he's likely to offer substantially less than its current list price. That, after all, is a retail price and dealers must purchase at wholesale in order to turn a profit.

Care to hold a personal treasure hunt? Here's a list of scarce coins—some worth hundreds of dollars—that might turn up in your pocket change today:

• The 1960 small-date Lincoln cents.

   Early in 1960, coin collectors noticed something strange about the new one-cent pieces coming out of the main mint in Philadelphia and the branch in Denver. The numbers in the date were perceptibly smaller on some of these cents than on others—and the "small-date" coins were significantly scarcer than those with larger numbers.

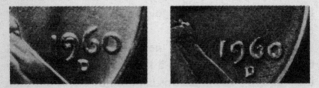

1960-D small- and large-date Lincoln cents. The close-up of the 6 on the left is the large date; the 6 on the right is the small date. The large date has the longer tail on the 6. (Photos courtesy Coin World)

As word of these "instant rarities" spread around the country, a coast-to-coast scavenger hunt ensued. The small-date cents from the Philadelphia Mint proved to be much more elusive than those from Denver. Before long, the price of these 1960-P cents (which carry no mint mark below the date) jumped to $400 for a roll of 50 coins. That's $8 apiece—a very tidy profit for those who obtained these coins at face value. The Denver small-date cents (with a D below the date) rose as high as $20 a roll, or 40 cents apiece, which is also nothing to sneeze at and also a nice return for those who invested just a penny and a little time.

The premiums on these coins have dropped with the passage of time. Still, both will bring you considerably more than a penny for your thoughts if you're fortunate enough to find them in circulation. The 1960-P small-date cent is now worth between $1 and $2 each, depending on its condition, while the 1960-D is worth between a nickel and a dime.

How can you tell a "small date" from a "large date"? The photos make the distinction clear. Take special note of the 6 on the small-date cent: It looks somewhat squashed and has a shorter upward tail than its large-date counterpart. Also, in the small date, the numbers seem farther apart. And the top of the 1 lines up with the top of the 9.

Cents in 1960 proof sets also came in both varieties, and again the small-date version was quite a bit scarcer. You'd have to pay about $25 today for a 1960 proof set with the small-date cent. That's $10 more than the price of the normal set with the large-date cent.

- The 1960-D cent with a small date punched over a large date.

   The cents of 1960 come in many varieties. This is one case where you'll need magnification. Under a glass, you'll note what appear to be slight double images in the numbers in the date. What you're actually seeing are numbers from both the "small date" and the "large date."

- The 1969-S doubled-die Lincoln cent.

   Earlier in this chapter, I wrote in some detail about
the double-image cents made by mistake in 1955 and
again in 1972 at the Philadelphia Mint. Those are coins
you should always be alert for, since both command
handsome premiums—and the 1972 cent, in particular,
may very well appear in your pocket or purse someday. (The chances of discovering the 1955 cent are
more remote since, as I noted earlier, the Lincoln cent's
design was modified in 1959 and coins produced before
that date are more likely to have been saved.)

   While these are the best-known examples of "doubled-
die" cents, they're not the only ones. Others exist—and
some of these come with similarly fancy price tags.

   One was made in 1969 at the San Francisco Mint (denoted by an S below the date). As with the 1955 and 1972
varieties, the features of this coin are doubled on only the
obverse (or "heads" side). The date and inscriptions on
this side of the coin display distinct doubling. You can
see this much more readily under a magnifying glass, and
I recommend that you buy one to assist you. It will come
in handy not only in identifying doubled-die coins but
also in spotting other mint errors and unusual varieties.
A 5-power glass is fine for most such purposes, and you
can obtain one for only a few dollars. You'll recoup this
small investment with a single worthwhile find.

   The 1969-S doubled-die cent would be a *very*
worthwhile find: Well-known coin dealer Harry J. Forman of Philadelphia is paying between $100 and $200
for typical examples of this coin. And Forman says he
would pay $1,000 for a really exceptional example.

- The 1970-S "Atheist" cent.

   The motto *IN GOD WE TRUST* has appeared on

U.S. coinage since 1864, when religious fervor born of the Civil War gave impetus to this and other expressions of the nation's collective belief in a supreme being. Not all coins carried the inscription right away; it didn't appear on the nickel, for example, until 1938. But it now has been a fixture on every U.S. coin for more than half a century.

The Lincoln cent has borne this familiar motto right from the start—since Abe Lincoln's penny first appeared on the scene in 1909. And the motto has a prominent place along the top of the obverse, right above Lincoln's head. There are, however, a few Lincoln cents on which the nation's trust in God is compromised. The result is both interesting and potentially profitable for lucky pocket-change treasure-hunters.

The compromise occurs because of mint errors which cause part of the motto to be missing. The best-known example of this took place in 1970 at the San Francisco Mint. Part of the metal on one or more of the obverse cent dies—the pieces of metal used to strike the "heads" side of the cent—broke off that year along the upper edge. As a result, that portion of the coin was covered by a "cud," or small lump of metal, instead of getting the imprint of the design. (Since the die metal was missing, the metal in the coin blank simply expanded and filled the empty area.) As luck would have it, the cud completely obliterated the words *WE TRUST* in the motto. Enterprising dealers soon dubbed this the "Atheist cent."

At one time, there was a lively market for Atheist cents and a brand new example would fetch $20 or more. The market isn't as active today—but, even so, a nice Atheist cent will bring about $5. Keep in mind

that the error occurred on San Francisco cents, which
have an S mint mark below the date.

- The 1970-S small-date Lincoln cent.

Small-date and large-date cents turned up again in
1970—this time on coins from the San Francisco Mint
(identified by an S below the date). As in 1960, they
appeared on both regular cents and proofs. And, once
more, the small-date coins proved to be scarcer and
more valuable.

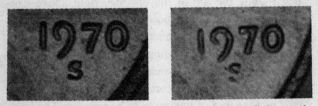

*1970-S small- and large-date Lincoln cents. The small date on the
right has the top of the 7 and the top of the 0 aligned. (Photos
courtesy Krause Publications)*

The 1970 small-date cents didn't create as much excitement initially as their predecessors had ten years earlier.
But, while the 1960 coins have dipped in value with time,
the 1970 versions appear to be getting more popular and
desirable. That's because collectors have determined that
fewer were made.

To get a 1970-S small-date cent from a coin dealer,
you'd have to pay about $17 each for the "business
strike"—the regular kind produced for circulation—and
$65 for the proof. However, there's a much cheaper way
to pick one up: Check the cents in that jar in your kitchen
cupboard! You're not very likely to find one of the proofs;
those were sold to collectors in custom-made plastic cases.

But the regular kind may very well turn up. And, if it does, you've made yourself close to $20!

As with the 1960 small-date cents, it may take a little time before you can tell the "small" 1970 dates from the "large" ones. But knowing how to spot them is your edge! That's what gives you the inside track over people who don't know the difference. To the untrained eye, these coins—and the scarce 1960 coins, too—blend in with all the other Lincoln cents in a cookie jar or cigar box. The trick is to develop a *trained* eye. And it's really an easy trick.

Take a close look at the photos I've provided. Focus, in particular, on the 7 in each of the dates. In the large date, the tops of the 9 and the 0 are higher than the top of the 7. In the small date, the tops of all four numbers look uniform.

- The 1971-S cent with a doubled-die obverse (or "heads" side).

  This has been far less publicized than the 1972 doubled-die cent described earlier in this chapter, and apparently is far rarer.
- The 1972-D cent without the designer's initials V.D.B.

  Cents without the V.D.B. turned up in significant quantities starting in 1988 (see pages 45–46). The same kind of error has also been discovered on 1972 cents minted in Denver (with a D below the date). These appear to be considerably rarer than those from the late 1980s.
- The 1979-D cent without the designer's initials FG.

  Frank Gasparro had a long and busy career at the U.S. Mint, where he was chief engraver for more than sixteen years. Besides designing the back of the Kennedy half dollar, he also created the Lincoln Memorial design used on the reverse of the current cent. And just as his initials have sometimes been omitted from Kennedy halves, they've also turned up missing on Lincoln cents. The letters "FG" are supposed to appear just to the right of the Lincoln Memorial's base. But in 1979, they were left off a few of the cents from the Denver Mint (identifiable by the D below the date).

• The 1980 D-over-S cent.

From time to time, more than one mint mark shows up on a coin—not in different places, but with one superimposed directly above the other. Sometimes this occurs because of misguided economy: In an effort to save a little money, an engraver at one of the mints may take an unused die made for use at the San Francisco Mint (with an S mint mark) and cut a D into the metal right above the S so the die can be used in Denver. Inevitably, an eagle-eyed collector will detect the original letter with a magnifying glass.

"Over-mint-mark" and "overdate" varieties are not routine; this kind of sloppiness is discouraged at the Mint—and when it does take place, the coins that result are eagerly pursued by many collectors. That, in turn, gives them considerable value.

Through the years, several such varieties have been found among Lincoln cents. Under a glass, you'll see that the D mint mark below the date is actually superimposed above an S. This coin is considered very scarce.

• The 1981 D-over-S cent.

The same thing happened again the following year. Only a microscopic trace remains of the original "S" mint mark.

• The 1982 small-date zinc cent.

Most people don't realize that the current one-cent

piece is made almost entirely out of zinc. It looks very much like the "copper" cent of yesteryear, but that's because it's plated with pure copper. The core of the coin is 99.2 percent zinc.

The Mint made the change in 1982 because the price of copper had risen to the point where the cent's metal value was approaching its value as money. Zinc is not only cheaper than copper but also lighter-weight, so more coins can be made from the same number of pounds.

The cent had contained zinc for more than a century; from 1864 to 1962, the coin's composition had been bronze (an alloy of copper, tin, and zinc), and since 1962 it had been brass (copper and zinc but no tin). But, in both those alloys, copper accounted for 95 percent of the weight. The present cent, by contrast, is 97.5 percent zinc and just 2.5 percent copper.

During the changeover year of 1982, brass and zinc cents were both produced in very substantial numbers. Both were made at Philadelphia (no mint mark) and also at Denver (a D below the date). And, to make matters even more interesting, the date that year came in both large and small varieties.

In all, there are seven different 1982 cent varieties: large-date brass cents from both Philadelphia and Denver ... small-date brass cents from Philadelphia ... and large- and small-date zinc cents from both mints. For some reason, small-date brass cents weren't made at the Denver Mint—but that was the only missing combination.

None of these varieties turned out to be extremely scarce. But the small-date zinc cent from the Philadelphia Mint is elusive, and coin dealers who specialize in cents are currently paying $25 a roll (or 50 cents per coin) for this variety.

How can you tell the difference? It's relatively easy to distinguish the large date from the small; there's a sharp variation in size. Telling brass from zinc isn't quite so simple, since outwardly the zinc cent looks pretty much like the brass. People who handle coins on a regular basis find the brass cents noticeably heavier, but the difference may not be as apparent to those with less experience.

Until you gain the expertise and confidence to tell the coins apart without external help, I recommend the purchase of a simple scale. For less than a dollar, you can obtain a penny scale marketed by the Whitman Coin Products division of Western Publishing Company (1220 Mound Ave., Racine, WI 53404). With a brass cent, the indicator will dip; with a zinc cent, it will stay up.

- The 1983 doubled-die Lincoln cent.

In 1983, another double-image cent appeared. This time, however, the doubling was on the reverse. Find one of these and you'll be not only seeing double but sitting pretty: Brand new, this coin now retails for about $200—and even in worn condition it's worth between $50 and $100.

Worth $200. *1983 doubled-die Lincoln cent. This blow-up shows the doubled letters on the reverse that make this coin scarce and sought-after. (Photo courtesy* Coin World)

One expert estimates that no more than 10,000 examples were produced. And most, he says, were released in the vicinity of Lancaster, Pennsylvania. Obviously, you should be especially watchful for this coin if you live within spending distance of that town.

- The 1984 cent without the initials FG.

    This coin is similar to the 1979-D cent described a few paragraphs earlier. It's not a great rarity, but it's worth a modest premium to mint-error specialists.
- The 1984 cent with a doubled obverse.

    This coin has attracted less publicity than the 1983 cent with the double-image reverse I just described. Nonetheless, it appears to be quite scarce; according to one expert, only about 2,000 have shown up. The doubling is clearest at Lincoln's ear and beard.

Worth $100. *1984 doubled-die Lincoln cent. The doubled ear is visible on the blow-up. (Photo courtesy* Coin World)

- Lincoln cents without the designer's initials V.D.B.

    At the start of this chapter, I mentioned that some Lincoln cents derive substantial value from the presence of the letters V.D.B. As I explained, these are the initials of Victor D. Brenner, the artist who designed this durable coin. It now turns out that the *absence* of these initials can also give a coin added value.

Before reviewing the reason, let's go back to 1909, the year the Lincoln cent was introduced. Brenner's initials, along the lower edge on the coin's reverse, caught the eye of many sharp observers—and more than a few objected to the size of this "signature." So many complained, in fact, that the Mint removed the letters within a matter of weeks.

In 1918, the initials were restored—but in much smaller letters and in a location where they wouldn't be nearly as conspicuous: at the base of Abraham Lincoln's shoulder. They've remained there ever since—or rather, they're *supposed* to be there. In 1988, collectors discovered a number of newly minted cents on which the initials were missing. Apparently, someone at the Mint inadvertently removed them while polishing one of the dies (the pieces of steel that impart the design to a coin, very much like cookie cutters).

The same thing happened again in 1989 and 1990. Pull out your magnifying glass and see if *you* can find some. If you do, there are dealers who will pay you upwards of $5 each. Please note, however, that the premiums will apply only to coins in brand new condition or very nearly so. Once Lincoln cents circulate for a while, the letters V.D.B. tend to wear down and wear off, and those coins naturally don't command a premium based on the absence of the initials.

• The 1939 Jefferson nickel with a doubled reverse.

Despite its age (more than fifty years old), this coin

has a good possibility of turning up in pocket change. That's because Jefferson nickels still have the same design and metallic composition today as they did when they first came out in 1938. You'll notice the doubling especially in the words *FIVE CENTS* and *MONTICELLO*. (Don't expect to see a dramatic double image in the building; the doubling isn't that obvious.) This coin is worth $10 or more even in well-worn condition.

- The 1949 D-over-S Jefferson nickel.

You'll certainly need a 5-power glass—and maybe even a 10-power glass—to pick out this rarity; after all, the letters are small and the people who cut the dies were trying to conceal the original mint mark. But, if you're successful in finding one of these coins, the reward can be great.

The 1949 D-over-S nickel was struck at the Denver Mint with a die originally meant for San Francisco. Look very closely and you'll see part of the S directly below the D. You'll also see dollar signs, for this coin can be worth more than $100 in nice condition.

- The 1954 S-over-D Jefferson nickel.

In 1954, the tables were turned: This time, a die made for Denver was recut for use in San Francisco. The S mint mark doesn't completely hide the original D— although, once again, you'll need a decent magnifying glass to detect this. The payoff this time will be a little less, since this coin appears to be more common. Even so, you'll pocket $10 or more—a lot more if the coin is unusually nice.

- The 1955 D-over-S Jefferson nickel.

In 1955, operations were halted at the San Francisco Mint, not to be resumed for more than a decade. Thus, the temptation was particularly strong to pull an unused San Francisco die off the shelf when the need arose for an extra die in Denver. After all, there wouldn't be any more need for the die in San Francisco.

Whatever the cause, the result was another crop of D-over-S nickels. These coins are approximately equal in scarcity and value to the S-over-D nickels from one year earlier.

- The 1964-D nickel with E PLURIDUS UNUM.

E PLURIBUS UNUM ("Out of many, one") is a motto that has graced U.S. coins for nearly two centuries. Once in a while, production problems lead to misspelling of this inscription. That's what happened in 1964 with Jefferson nickels made at the Denver Mint (with a D just to the right of Monticello on the reverse). Heavy polishing of one or more of the dies caused the center of the letter "B" to be obliterated. As a result, the word looks like PLURIDUS instead of PLURIBUS. This isn't an extremely valuable error, but it's certainly an interesting one—and it does command a modest premium.

- The 1983-D nickel with a doubled reverse.

Again, here's a coin with doubling of some of the features—this time on the reverse. The double image is relatively weak on this 1983 nickel from the Denver Mint (with a D just below and just to the left of the date on the "heads" side). Still, it's worth a premium to dealers and collectors who specialize in this type of error.

- The 1964 dime struck in copper-nickel.

The rising price of silver forced the U.S. government to discontinue production of silver dimes and quarters starting in 1965. Since then, these coins have been made from an alloy of copper and nickel bonded to a core of pure copper. All dimes and quarters minted during 1964 were made of silver—or rather, they were *supposed* to have been. But experiments with the new "clad" coinage were already under way at that time, and somehow a few dimes dated 1964 were made of copper-nickel, rather than silver. These are extremely rare and quite valuable. Hint: Look for a coppery reddish line around the rim of the coin; if it's there, the chances are good that you've found a "clad" coin, rather than a silver one.

- The 1967 dime with a doubled obverse.

Again, the Mint produced a coin with a double image, this time on the "heads" side. It's uncertain where this 1967 dime was produced; from 1965 through 1967, the Mint withheld mint marks in order to discourage hoarding of coins by speculators. In any event, the coin is quite scarce. The doubling is most apparent on the mottos and the date.

- The 1970-D dime with a doubled reverse.

By 1970, mint marks had been restored—and a double-image error was in evidence once again. This 1970 dime from the Denver Mint (with a D just above the date) has doubling on the reverse.

- The 1982 no-P Roosevelt dime.

Up until recent years, coins that were made at the Philadelphia Mint almost never carried a mint mark. "P-mint" coins were distinguished not by a special letter, but rather by the *absence* of any such letter. But, since 1980, a tiny letter P has been stamped on all Philly coins except the cent.

Worth $100. *1982 no-P Roosevelt dime. (Photo courtesy* Coin World*)*

As you might expect, this has given rise to errors now and then when the P has been omitted. One such error occurred in 1982, when collectors began to notice Philadelphia dimes without the mint mark. This error proved embarrassing for the Mint—but make no mistake, it can be a real bonanza for people like you: A typical example will bring you between $25 and $100.

- The 1965 quarter struck in silver.

  This is the flip side of the dime error I listed a few coins back. In that case, a 1964 dime was *supposed* to be silver but was made of copper-nickel instead. In 1965, all dimes and quarters were supposed to be made of copper-nickel—but a very small number of quarters got minted in silver by mistake. This is a rare and valuable coin. Unlike "clad" coins, it *won't* have a reddish line around the rim.
- The 1970 quarter with a doubled reverse.

  Once more, a double-image error appeared in 1970—this time on quarters from the Philadelphia Mint (struck without a mint mark near the lower right corner of the "heads" side, behind George Washington's pigtail). The doubling is visible only on the coin's reverse, and you'll need a magnifying glass to detect it.

• The 1970-D quarter with a doubled reverse.

Double-image reverses turned up in 1970 on quarters from the Denver Mint as well (this time with a D mint mark behind Washington's pigtail). There are quite a few different varieties of this particular error.

• The 1977-D silver-clad quarter.

In 1975 and 1976, the Mint made special part-silver versions of the Washington quarter, Kennedy half dollar, and Eisenhower dollar. These were sold to collectors at a premium. Production of these 40-percent-silver coins was discontinued after 1976—or rather, it was *supposed* to have been. But in 1977, a few quarters were made at the Denver Mint (with a D mint mark behind the pigtail) on leftover silver-clad (40-percent-silver) coin blanks. These are extremely rare and valuable.

• The 1989 no-P Washington quarter.

The P mint mark went astray again in 1989 on a small number of quarters. (The mint mark should appear behind George Washington's pigtail, near the bottom of the obverse). And this time the error drew national attention, thanks to a Page One story in *The New York Times*.

Worth $40. *1989 no-P Washington quarter (bottom). Not a recognized variety, but still a curiosity. (Photo courtesy Miller Magazines, Inc.)*

As with several other important mint errors, this one turned up in the largest quantities in Pennsylvania, especially the Pittsburgh area. An obvious explanation is the fact that the mint itself is in that state, and these are early stops in the distribution chain. Multiple findings also were reported in North Carolina.

Coin dealer Harry Forman, himself a Pennsylvanian, touted this coin on the television program "Hidden Rewards." A number of lucky viewers who checked their change afterward found "no-P" quarters and shipped them off to Forman to claim their rewards—which were no longer hidden. The longtime Philadelphia dealer has purchased dozens of these coins at prices ranging from $10 to $100 apiece.

• The 1964 half dollar with a doubled obverse.

The Kennedy half dollar drew international attention when it first appeared in 1964, soon after the assassination of President John F. Kennedy. Admirers of the slain president—not only in the United States but all around the world—rushed to obtain examples of the coin as Kennedy mementos. Only sharp-eyed collectors noticed that some of those very first Kennedy half dollars had doubling on the obverse (or "heads" side). You may very well have one sitting in a drawer or cigar box even now!

- The 1964 half dollar with a doubled reverse.

Some 1964 Kennedy half dollars have doubling on the *reverse*, rather than the obverse. Get out your magnifying glass to look for this variety; it won't jump right out at you. But you'll spot it right away under the glass.

- The 1966 half dollar without the designer's initials FG.

The Lincoln cent isn't the only coin discovered on occasion without its designer's initials. Eagle-eyed hobbyists have discovered that on some Kennedy half dollars, the letters FG are missing from their designated spot just to the right of the eagle's tail near the base of the coin's reverse. These are the initials of Frank Gasparro, the engraver who designed this side of the coin.

As in the case of cents without the "V.D.B.," this omission resulted from overzealous polishing of one or more dies (the pieces of metal used to strike the coins).

This error has been discovered on coins from a number of years and from different mints. Most don't seem to be excessively rare, but the 1966 is one of the scarcest. Relatively few examples are known with this date.

Half dollars without the designer's initials are not world-class mint errors; some, in fact, might argue that the error is trivial. But don't let that discourage you from looking: If you find one, you can sell it to a small army of dedicated enthusiasts—including Harry Forman—for several dollars.

- The 1972-D half dollar without the designer's initials FG.

    The letters FG are missing on a small number of 1972 Kennedy halves from the Denver Mint (with a D below JFK's neckline on the "heads" side). These 1972-D error coins appear to be much scarcer than later ones.

- The 1973 half dollar without the initials FG.

    Here we go again! While you're checking Kennedy half dollars for Frank Gasparro's initials, make a special point of examining those dated 1973. This is another instance where some were made without them.

- The 1974-D half dollar with a doubled obverse.

    Another double-image error occurred in 1974, this time on Kennedy half dollars from the Denver Mint (with a D below Kennedy's neckline on the "heads" side). The doubling occurs only on the obverse and is plainest on the mottos. This appears to be a rare variety.

- The 1982 Kennedy half dollar without the designer's initials.

    The 1982 half dollar without the letters FG was the first to receive widespread publicity. Similar error coins had been known before that, but hadn't really attracted much attention. When the 1982 coins became popular, collectors took a closer look at earlier half dollars and discovered—or rediscovered—several others. At present, the 1982 is worth about $5.

- Any silver coins.

    In 1965, with silver rising in price, the U.S. Treasury sought and obtained permission from Congress to change the composition of the coins it was producing in that metal. Under the legislation, new dimes and quarters were made with no silver at all, while the half dollar's silver content was reduced. (In 1971, the last trace of silver was removed from that coin, too.)

As you might expect, the American public responded with a nationwide silver rush, pulling silver coins out of circulation. Within a few years, hardly any remained—and today, a silver coin is an uncommon sight indeed among the copper-nickel dimes, quarters, and halves in our pockets and purses.

But, while seldom seen, silver coins do turn up from time to time—and those who are actively *looking* for these coins are the ones most likely to *see* them. At one time, in the early 1980s, silver was worth about $50 an ounce. Its value has declined considerably since then. But, even so, any silver coin you find in pocket change will bring you a healthy profit. As this is written, silver bullion is valued at approximately $5 an ounce, so any "traditional" silver U.S. coin (with a silver content of 90 percent) will be worth about five times its face value. The value of silver coins, of course, goes up proportionally as silver itself rises in price.

COINS NOT TO LOOK FOR

Some coins that seem unusual when they turn up in pocket change are really not worth your time or trouble. Although they are not encountered every day, they are actually quite common and have little or no premium value as collectibles. These coins may bring a premium in higher Mint State grades, but in lesser condition they're worth very little.

Here are a few coins *not* to look for:

- Susan B. Anthony dollars.

  Except for the scarce 1979 variety with the "clear-S" mint mark, Anthony dollars are generally worth no more than face value: one dollar each. It's true that these much disliked coins haven't been produced since 1981. However, the Mint pumped out almost 900 million examples in 1979 and 1980, many of which remain in government vaults.
- Eisenhower dollars.

  A few of the Eisenhower dollars minted between 1971 and 1978 are in demand as collector's items. But, with these exceptions, "Ike" dollars are just about as common as the Susan B. Anthony dollars that took their place.
- Kennedy half dollars dated after 1970.

  From 1964 to 1970, Kennedy half dollars contained silver. The amount of precious metal was reduced beginning in 1965—but, even so, Kennedy halves from any of these years have bonus value based on the price of silver. Since 1971, virtually all half dollars have been made of a copper-nickel alloy—the same one used to make quarters and dimes. The only exceptions were the special collector's items sold in conjunction with the nation's Bicentennial in 1975–76. These coins may not be encountered very often, but they're certainly worth saving.
- Business-strike Bicentennial coins.

  While relatively small quantities of the three Bicentennial coins—the Washington quarter, Kennedy half dollar, and Eisenhower dollar—were struck in silver for sale to collectors at a premium, the vast majority of these coins are regular "business-strike" pieces made of copper-nickel alloy. These may catch your eye when they pop up in change now and then, but they're neither scarce nor valuable.

- "Wheat-ears" Lincoln cents.

As noted earlier, the reverse of the Lincoln cent underwent a design change in 1959. As a consequence, cents with the old design—featuring two simple wheat stalks on the reverse—gradually came to be less common in Americans' pocket change. Today, these "wheat-ears" cents are relatively scarce in circulation. But that doesn't mean they're scarce in an absolute sense: Many millions have been saved by collectors and hoarders. These coins do enjoy a very small premium; you could probably sell a roll of 50 common-date wheat-ears cents for a dollar or two. But that hardly justifies an all-out search for these coins.

- The 1974 aluminum cent.

Another coin you shouldn't bother looking for is the 1974 aluminum cent. In this case, however, it's not because the coin is unduly common: It is, in fact, a rarity which any red-blooded collector would love to own. There are two reasons not to bother looking: First, you almost certainly won't find one; and second, even if you did find one, Uncle Sam would seize it if he found out.

In the early 1970s, a growing shortage of cents—and the rising price of copper—prompted the U.S. Mint to explore alternative metals for our nation's lowest-value coin. It settled upon aluminum as the most likely substitute and actually proceeded with production of considerable quantities—reportedly in the neighborhood of 1 million pieces. But Congress declined to authorize this switch and the Mint was obliged to abandon the idea.

There was just one complication: During the time it was seeking support in Congress for the plan, the Mint

sent samples of the new aluminum cents to various
senators and congressmen—and some of these coins
never found their way back. Even today, some are un-
accounted for. However, Mint officials have made it
clear that since the aluminum cents were never officially issued, any that might turn up would be subject
to confiscation by the U.S. Secret Service.

LESS THAN MINT

Just as there are certain coins you shouldn't waste your
time looking for in pocket change, there also are coins
you shouldn't waste your money buying. Modern coins
and coin sets sold at a premium by government or private
mints are high on this list of items to avoid.

In recent years, the United States Mint has made and
marketed dozens of commemorative coins. These are
coins authorized by Congress to honor some special person, place, or event. Typically, they are produced in limited quantities and offered for sale at a premium many
times their face value and also well above the value of
the metal they contain (generally silver or gold). With
few exceptions, these coins have been very poor per-
formers in the resale market. They tend to fall in price after their initial sale by the Mint, and within a few years
almost all have market values below their issue price—
often well below. In part, this is because the issue prices
usually include substantial surcharges earmarked for the
benefit of organizations sponsoring these coinage programs. The United States Olympic Committee has been a
beneficiary several times, for example.

If your purpose in buying coins is to realize a profit,

you would be wise to steer clear of commemoratives when the U.S. Mint offers them for sale. For that matter, new-issue coins and coin sets sold by *any* mint—government or private, domestic or foreign—have amassed a poor track record, by and large, in recent years. The annual proof sets and "mint sets" sold by Uncle Sam are very much in the group of items to avoid. Like U.S. commemorative coins, they have tended to fall in value—often sharply—in the secondary market.

UNCONVENTIONAL WISDOM

Serious numismatists—dedicated coin collectors—sometimes make light of "pocket-change rarities." A feeling exists within a certain segment of the hobby that coins found in ordinary pocket change are somehow less significant than beautiful, pristine pieces that never entered everyday circulation. With all due respect to those who hold this view, I feel that on the contrary, coins that have "been around" gain added appeal from having seen actual use.

Most coins (excluding proofs) are made to be spent, so these pieces have served their intended function. And while it's always exciting to own an exceptional coin, there's a special satisfaction—an undeniable thrill—in finding a worthwhile coin in circulation. It's very much like digging up buried treasure.

Pocket-change rarities may not have fancy pedigrees, but many do command fancy prices. And they're definitely out there, waiting to be found. Interesting and valuable coins are turning up in pocket change every day. And more will turn up tomorrow.

So start looking—and happy hunting!

CHAPTER 3

MAKING MONEY
WITH COINS

Treasure doesn't always come in a massive oak chest buried by pirates on a lush tropical island. It can also be found in an ordinary cigar box tucked away in a corner of your attic.

If you find such a box and it's filled with old coins, it may very well be worth a small fortune—and possibly even a big one.

I'll give you an example.

One day in the late 1970s, a man walked into a Boston coin store. The man had inherited a group of old coins from his father, and he didn't have the foggiest notion what they were or how much they were worth. These coins had been stored in the attic for thirty or forty years, in little cardboard boxes stuffed with cotton.

They turned out to be original sets of proof coins, purchased from the United States Mint in the late 1800s and early 1900s by the father, who had been a collector. And they proved to be a bonanza for the son.

"These coins had a face value of probably seventy or eighty dollars, and the man had no idea they were worth any more than that," said Jim Halperin, then the chief executive of that Boston coin firm. "Upon my recommendation, he consigned them to one of our auctions and they realized nearly half a million dollars."

This story is not unique. Rare coins have brought handsome profits to many millions of people who found or bought the coins themselves or acquired them from family members or friends. These lucky individuals have included people from every stratum of society—rich and poor, young and old, the powerful and famous, and the ordinary man and woman in the street.

Everyday people reap windfalls from coins all the time, and often they obtain those coins in unpredictable ways.

Steve Ivy, now a business partner of Halperin's in the hugely successful Heritage Rare Coin Galleries of Dallas, tells of a man who bought an old silver dollar from a drinking companion in a bar in Eureka, California. Neither knew the value of the coin; both considered it just a conversation piece. So the friend sold the coin to the man for just a dollar. A while later, the buyer received some literature from Heritage; his name had wound up on a mailing list used by the firm. He got in touch with the company and asked about his coin.

His $1 purchase turned out to be a great rarity—a silver dollar minted in 1870 in San Francisco. He placed it in one of Ivy's auctions and it realized more than $30,000.

PRICE PERFORMANCE

Coin prices tend to follow a boom-and-bust cycle, rising in value sharply, then going down in price almost as sharply, sometimes within a period of just a couple of months. Over the long term, however, many truly rare coins have enjoyed phenomenal price growth—and sustained it.

Coins are popular not only because sometimes they might appreciate in value, but also because they can be appreciated for what they are: timeless works of hand-held art that mirror the history of man. People like to look at them, admire their beauty, and ponder the role they played in the drama of civilization.

Truly rare coins sometimes go up in value even during periods when the coin market as a whole is in a slump. Dramatic evidence came in October 1993, when a 1913 Liberty Head nickel—one of five known examples of this great U.S. rarity—changed hands at a New York City auction for $962,500. The seller, prominent Texas numismatist Reed Hawn, had bought the coin in 1985 for $385,000. Thus, he more than doubled his money in less than a decade, even though he sold the coin in a hostile market environment.

Coin prices got an artificial boost in the late 1980s when major Wall Street brokerage firms pumped millions of dollars in new investment money into rare coins. Merrill Lynch and Kidder, Peabody both established limited partnerships tied to investments in coins, and together these funds injected tens of millions of dollars into the coin market—including significant sums from people who had never bought coins before. The new money, combined with anticipation of even more, sent coin prices soaring; in the spring of 1989, many were at or near all-time highs.

Unfortunately, the timing was bad. Like much of the U.S. economy, the coin market soured during the recession of the early 1990s. Making matters worse, the Federal Trade Commission—drawn by Wall Street's involvement—found and publicized evidence of wrongdoing by certain unscrupulous elements in the coin market, and this frightened many investors away. The brokerage firms retreated as well, leaving longer-established coin buyers and sellers with only bittersweet memories of this whirlwind courtship and leaving the rare coin marketplace itself in disarray. Eventually, well-known California entrepreneur Bruce McNall pleaded guilty to fraud in connection with his role as manager of Merrill Lynch's Athena II rare-coin fund. Those who invested in that fund fared better, however: The brokerage agreed to compensate them in full for their losses. One of the law firms litigating the case against Merrill Lynch hired me as an expert numismatic consultant, so I had the satisfaction of helping these people recover their money.

In the eyes of many outsiders, this whole unhappy episode dimmed rare coins' luster as an investment vehicle. But those with longer perspectives and closer ties to the coin market know that this affair was an aberration. Rare coins should not be viewed as shooting stars; they are steady, solid stores of value, and if they are purchased wisely, treated well, and held for the longer term, they might well bring their owner a profit. They may not perform as spectacularly as they did in the 1980s, when outside influences drove their prices up unrealistically, but their long-range track record has been excellent. In fact, it was that record—documented in annual reports issued by the Salomon Brothers investment firm—that caught Wall Street's attention in the first place. Those reports showed that, over a twenty-year period beginning in the late 1960s, rare coins had outperformed all other investment vehicles measured by the firm, including stocks and bonds.

Many savvy investors considered rare coins a good buy in the late 1980s. Events proved them wrong in the

short term. But if those shrewd buyers liked the investment potential of coins priced at $5,000 apiece, it cer-
tainly seems reasonable to look upon those coins as even
better values today, now that they're available for just a
few hundred dollars. Wall Street's marriage with the rare
coin market ended in a quickie divorce, but rare coins
were doing fine long before Wall Street came into their
life, and we hope that they'll prosper once again now that
they're on their own.

THE CERTIFIED ADVANTAGE

If you find any Mint State or proof examples of coins no
longer seen in circulation, I advise you to have them certified by a reputable, independent third-party grading service. As this book is being written, the leading services
are the Numismatic Guaranty Corporation of America
(NGC), the Professional Coin Grading Service (PCGS),
and ANACS. Having your coins certified will not only
enhance their marketability, but also provide them with
tamper-resistant holders.

In years gone by, a number of people who purchased
or found rare coins ended up selling them for less than
their fair market value. They would go to a dealer and offer their coins for sale and the dealer would tell them,
"This coin is fairly common; I'll give you five dollars for
it." And the dealer would then turn around and sell the
coin for hundreds—or even thousands—of dollars.

Today, we have organizations that help protect collectors, and the populace at large, against such abuse.

A coin encapsulated by the Professional Coin Grading Service.
(Photo courtesy PCGS)

They're known as independent coin-grading services, and they serve in a real sense as watchdogs for the coin-collecting public. For a modest fee, these services examine coins that are sent to them for review, then render expert judgments concerning the grade of each coin—its level of preservation—on a 1 to 70 scale. This, in turn, gives the consumer a good idea of how much her coin is worth, since grade is a key determinant of price. Each coin is returned in a sonically sealed, hard plastic holder, along with a paper tab stating its grade.

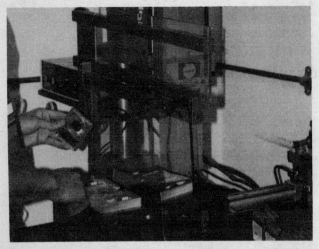

Coin holder being sonically sealed in the PCGSs encapsulation room. (Photo courtesy PCGS)

These grading organizations have no vested interest in the coins they are examining. Thus, the consumer can have the utmost confidence in their judgments.

Consumers with coins that appear on the list at the end of this chapter should give serious consideration to having these coins certified. I would urge without hesitation that any such coins be independently certified before being offered for sale.

Most coin dealers are knowledgeable and reliable, and will pay fair value for any coins offered to them for sale. However, there's always a chance that you may be unlucky and end up dealing with someone less fair and honest. Having your coins certified will help protect you against that possibility.

Certification also provides you with a safe holder in which to store your coin. If you choose not to have your coins certified, I'll give you some tips at the end of this chapter on how to safely hold and house your coins.

COINS TO LOOK FOR

By now, perhaps you've tracked down some old coins in a desk or dresser drawer, or maybe in that cigar box in the attic. Naturally, you're curious to know whether any of these are valuable—and, if so, how much they're worth.

I don't propose to offer you a comprehensive list of every United States coin ever minted. Rather, I've selected the scarcest and most valuable coins from each series and shown the market value for each of these coins—coins, with few exceptions, which have a realistic chance of turning up in that long-forgotten cigar box.

Some U.S. coins of extraordinary value don't appear on this list, primarily because there's little or no chance of finding them. Many other coins with modest premium value are likewise omitted. I know you're not really interested in whether your coins are worth 10 or 25 cents—or even a dollar or two—more than their face value. You want to know whether you've hit it big.

First-year-of-issue coins have always been widely saved, so these are quite likely to turn up in your holdings. People tend to set aside examples of new coins in the year they first appear; consequently, such coins are often found years later in very high levels of preservation. But this doesn't mean that first-year-of-issue coins can't be scarce and valuable. Take the 1909-S V.D.B. Lincoln cent, for example. This is a first-year coin, yet a Mint State example can be worth $2,500—and you may very well find just such a coin in your personal treasure trove.

Treat this list as a guide. If you find you have several coins that appear in this compilation, chances are good that what you actually have is a carefully assembled collection—one that may be worth a lot of money. If so, I advise you to seek more information from a professional. In fact, if you have *many* of the rare-date coins that are listed here, feel free to contact the author directly: Scott Travers Rare Coin Galleries Inc., F.D.R. Box 1711, New York, NY 10150.

For more detailed pricing information on U.S. coinage as a whole, and additional historical details, there are four yearly price-guide books that many find helpful: my own book, *The Insider's Guide to U.S. Coin Values* (Bantam Doubleday Dell, yearly); *The Official* Blackbook Price Guide of United States Coins by Marc Hudgeons (House of Collectibles, yearly); *A Guide Book of United States Coins* by R.S. Yeoman, edited by Kenneth Bressett (Western Publishing Company, yearly); and the *Coin World Guide to U.S. Coins, Prices & Value Trends*, written by William T. Gibbs and edited by Beth Deisher, with Trends values by Keith M. Zaner (Signet New American Library.

The values given here are for average circulated examples—coins that have passed from hand to hand and display significant wear. These prices correspond to coins that would be graded Fine-12. For further information about grading, turn to Chapter Six.

These are *fair market values*—the prices that would be paid in a retail transaction by a buyer with reasonable knowledge of the market, and the prices that would be charged by a seller under no undue duress to consummate the sale.

You won't necessarily be able to walk into your neighborhood shop and buy any of the coins listed here at these values—or be able, on the other hand, to sell any of the coins listed here at these values. This market is a volatile one, and the prices listed here could change substantially between the date of preparation of this list and the time you actually read this compilation.

Liberty Cap Half Cents (1793–1797)
(Coins valued at $1,000 or more in average circulated condition)

1793 (head facing left)	$ 3,000
1796 with pole behind Miss Liberty	9,000
1796 without pole	19,000
1797 with lettered edge	1,200

Draped Bust Half Cents (1800–1808)
(Coins valued at $1,000 or more in average circulated condition)

1802/0 with the reverse design of 1800 Draped Bust half cent. (Photo courtesy Auctions by Bowers and Merena, Inc.)

1802/0 (with the 2 engraved over a 0)	1,100
1802/0 with the reverse design of 1800	28,250
1805 with a small 5 and stars	1,250

Flowing Hair Large Cents (1793)
(All are valuable)

1793 Flowing Hair cent with chain reverse	4,800
1793 Flowing Hair cent (either plain or lettered edge) with wreath reverse	1,200
1793 Flowing Hair cent with wreath reverse and strawberry leaves above the date	80,000

Liberty Cap Large Cents (1793–1796)
(Coins valued at $1,000 or more in average circulated condition)

1793	3,000
1794 with the head of 1793	1,500
1794 with starred reverse	17,500
1795 with Jefferson head and plain edge	12,000

Draped Bust Large Cents (1796–1807)
(Coins valued at $1,000 or more in average circulated condition)

1799	3,000
1799/8 (with the 9 engraved over an 8)	4,250
1803 with large date and small fraction 1/100	4,500
1804	1,200
1807/6 (with the 7 engraved over a 6) with a small 7	4,500

Classic Head Large Cents (1808–1814)
(Coins valued at $250 or more in average circulated condition)

1809	300
1811	250
1811/0 (with the second 1 engraved over a 0)	250

Coronet Large Cents (1816–1857)
(These coins are much more common than earlier large cents. The following coins are valued at $100 or more in average circulated condition.)

1821	100
1823	200
1823/2 (with the 3 engraved over a 2)	175
1824/2 (with the 4 engraved over a 2)	100
1826/5 (with the 6 engraved over a 5)	100
1834 with large 8 and stars and medium letters	200
1839/6 (with the 9 engraved over a 6)	500

Flying Eagle Cents (1856–1858)

1856 Flying Eagle cent, Mint State. (Photo courtesy Auctions by Bowers and Merena, Inc.)

1856	2,500
1857	14
1858, both small-letters and large-letters varieties	14
1858 with the second 8 struck over a 7	150

Indian Head Cents (1859–1909)
(Coins valued at $25 or more in average circulated condition)

1864-L Indian head cent, Proof. (Photo courtesy Auctions by Bowers and Merena, Inc.)

1864 with the designer's initial L visible on the headdress	50
1866	34
1867	34
1868	33
1869	70
1869 with the last 9 recut (over another 9)	200
1870	60
1871	65
1872	70
1873 with the 3 closed	34
1873 with the word LIBERTY doubled	300
1876	25
1877	325
1878	30
1908-S (with an S below the wreath)	25
1909-S	125

Lincoln Cents (1909–present)
(Coins valued at $20 or more in
average circulated condition)

1909-S V.D.B. Lincoln cent, Mint State. (Photo courtesy Auctions by Bowers and Merena, Inc.)

1909-S V.D.B. (with an S below the date and V.D.B. at the base of the reverse)	350
1909-S (without the V.D.B.)	40
1914-D (with a D below the date)	80
1922 Plain (without the D below the date)	275
1931-S	28
1944-D/S (with a D engraved over the S below the date)	75

1955 doubled die (with doubling on the lettering on the front of the coin)	250
1972 doubled die (with doubling on the lettering on the front of the coin)	75

Two-Cent Pieces (1864–1873)
(Coins valued at $50 or more in average circulated condition)

1864 with small motto IN GOD WE TRUST	60
1869/8 (with the 9 engraved over an 8)	275
1872	100

Copper-Nickel Three-Cent Pieces (1865–1889)
(Coins valued at $20 or more in average circulated condition)

1885 Copper-nickel three-cent piece, Proof. (Photo courtesy Auctions by Bowers and Merena, Inc.)

1876	20
1879	50
1880	70
1882	68
1883	150
1884	250
1885	375
1887	225
1888	50
1889	70

Silver Three-Cent Pieces (1851–1873)
*(Coins valued at $20 or more in
average circulated condition)*

1851-O (with an O to the right of the Roman numeral III on the reverse)	25
1854	20
1855	25
1856	20
1857	20
1858	20
1859	20
1860	20
1861	20
1862/1 (with the 2 engraved over a 1)	22
1862	20

Flowing Hair Half Dimes (1792–1795)
*(Coins valued at $1,000 or more in
average circulated condition)*

1792	5,000
1794	1,200
1795	1,000

Draped Bust/Small Eagle Half Dimes (1796–1797)
*(Coins valued at $1,000 or more in
average circulated condition)*

1796/5 (with the 6 engraved over a 5)	1,100
1796	1,050
1796 with LIBERTY spelled LIKERTY	1,150
1797 with 15 stars	1,100
1797 with 16 stars	1,150
1797 with 13 stars	1,300

Draped Bust/Heraldic Eagle Half Dimes (1800–1805)
*(Coins valued at $1,000 or more in
average circulated condition)*

1802	23,000

Seated Liberty Half Dimes (1837–1873)
*(Coins valued at $100 or more in
average circulated condition)*

*1863 Seated Liberty half dime, Mint State. (Photo courtesy
Auctions by Bowers and Merena, Inc.)*

1838-O with no stars (with an O below the wreath on the reverse)	125
1839-O with a large O	400
1844-O	150
1846	190
1853-O with no arrows beside the date	175
1863	125
1864	285
1865	240
1866	200
1867	325

Shield Nickels (1866–1883)
*(Coins valued at $20 or more in
average circulated condition)*

*1867 Shield nickel, Proof. (Photo courtesy Scott Travers Rare
Coin Galleries, Inc.)*

1867 with rays	22
1871	40
1873 with the 3 closed	30
1877	1,000
1878	500
1879	250
1880	260
1881	200
1883/2 (with the 3 engraved over a 2)	60

(Most common dates are worth $10 in Fine-12.)

Liberty Head Nickels (1883–1912)
(Coins valued at more than $20 in Fine-12 condition)

1886 Liberty Head nickel, Proof. (Photo courtesy Scott Travers Rare Coin Galleries, Inc.)

1885	300
1886	75
1912-S (with an S below the dot to the left of the word CENTS on the reverse)	50
1913 (not an official mint issue; only 5 known. A proof specimen sold for $962,500 in October 1993)	500,000

Buffalo Nickels (1913–1938)
(Coins valued at $20 or more in average circulated condition)

1913-D Variety 2 (with the buffalo on flat ground and a D below the words FIVE CENTS)	40

1913-S Variety 2 (with the buffalo on flat ground
  and an S below the words FIVE CENTS)   90
1914-D   40
1915-S   20
1916 with doubling visible   1,100
1918/17-D (with the 8 engraved over a 7)   700
1921-S   40
1937-D with only three legs on the buffalo   100

(Most common dates are worth 75 cents in Fine-12.)

Jefferson Nickels (1938–present)
*(Coins valued at $20 or more in
average circulated condition)*

Worth $30. *1943-over-2 Jefferson Nickel. (Photo courtesy* Coin World*)*

1939 doubled die (with doubling in the words
  MONTICELLO and FIVE CENTS)   25
1943/2 (with the 3 engraved over a 2)   30
1943-P doubled die (with a large P over the dome of
  Monticello on the reverse)   25
1949-D/S (with the D mint mark, to the right of
  Monticello, engraved over an S)   20

Draped Bust/Small Eagle Dimes (1796–1797)
*(Coins valued at $1,000 or more in
average circulated condition)*

*1797 with 13 stars Draped Bust/small eagle dime. (Photo courtesy
Auctions by Bowers and Merena, Inc.)*

1796 with small eagle	1,500
1797 with 16 stars	1,100
1797 with 13 stars	1,100

Draped Bust/Heraldic Eagle Dimes (1798–1807)
*(Coins valued at $1,000 or more in
average circulated condition)*

1798/7 with 13 stars (with the 8 engraved over a 7)	1,500
1802	1,075
1804	1,500

Capped Bust Dimes (1809–1837)
*(Coins valued at $100 or more in
average circulated condition)*

1809	300
1811/9 (with the final 1 engraved over a 9)	100
1814 small date	100
1822	500
1829 with a curl-base 2	4,950

Seated Liberty Dimes (1837–1891)
*(Coins valued at $100 or more in
average circulated condition)*

*1874-CC with arrows beside the date Seated Liberty dime, Mint
State. (Photo courtesy Auctions by Bowers and Merena, Inc.)*

1839-O with the reverse of 1838 (with an O below the wreath on the reverse)	200
1843-O	100
1846	105
1858-S (with an S below the wreath)	100
1860-O	500
1863	325
1864	300
1865	410
1866	400
1867	420
1871-CC (with the letters CC below the wreath)	700
1872-CC	500
1873-CC with arrows beside the date	1,000
1874-CC with arrows beside the date	1,800
1879	185
1880	140
1881	140
1885-S	250

Barber Dimes (1892–1916)
*(Coins valued at $20 or more in
average circulated condition)*

*1894-S Barber dime, Proof. (Photo courtesy Auctions by Bowers
and Merena, Inc.)*

1892-S (with an S below the wreath)	30
1893-O (with an O below the wreath)	30
1894	30
1894-O	60
1894-S (unauthorized; 24 manufactured by the mint; last example realized $275,000)	10,000
1895	135
1895-O	250
1895-S	30
1896-S	60
1897-O	70
1901-S	60
1903-S	50
1904-S	45
1913-S	20

Winged Liberty Head (or "Mercury") Dime (1916–1945)
*(Coins valued at $20 or more in
average circulated condition)*

*1916-D Mercury dime, Mint State. (Photo courtesy Auctions by
Bowers and Merena, Inc.)*

1916-D (with a D to the right of ONE on the
  reverse)   700
1921   50
1921-D   80
1942/1 (with the 2 engraved over a 1)   200

Worth $200. *1942-over-1 Mercury dime. (Photo courtesy Bill Fivaz)*

1942/1-D (with the 2 engraved over a 1 and a D to
  the right of ONE on the reverse)   220

Twenty-Cent Pieces (1875–1878)
*(Coins valued at $20 or more in
Fine-12 condition)*

1875	60
1875-CC (with the letters CC below the eagle)	65
1875-S	50
1876	100
1876-CC (only 12 to 15 known)	8,500

(The 1877 and 1878 twenty-cent pieces are proof-only issues, generally worth several thousand dollars or more.)

Early Quarters (1796–1807)

1796, with small eagle	5,000
1804, with heraldic eagle	2,000
1805	375
1806/5 (with the 6 engraved over a 5)	300
1806	375
1807	310

Capped Bust Quarters (1815–1837)
(Every coin in this series is worth $20 or more in Fine-12 condition. The following coins are worth $100 or more.)

1815	100
1818/5 (with the second 8 engraved over a 5)	110
1818	100
1822	110
1824/2 (with the 4 engraved over a 2)	110
1825/2 (with the 5 engraved over a 2)	110

Seated Liberty Quarters (1838–1891)
(Every coin in this series is worth $20 or more in Fine-12 condition. The following dates are worth $100 or more.)

1842 large date	100
1842 small date	600
1843-O with a large O below the eagle on the reverse	140
1849-O	500
1851-O	200
1852-O	150
1853 over 53, with a recut date	150
1854-O with a huge O	100
1857-S	100
1858-S	100
1859-S	110
1860-S	100
1861-S	100
1865-S	100
1866 with the motto IN GOD WE TRUST	300
1866-S	200
1867	200
1867-S	150
1868-S	100
1869-S	150
1871-CC	1,000
1871-S	200
1872-CC	400
1872-S	300

1873 with a closed 3	120
1873-CC with arrows beside the date	1,500

1873-CC with arrows beside the date Seated Liberty quarter, Mint State. (Photo courtesy Auctions by Bowers and Merena, Inc.)

1875-CC	100
1878-S	120
1879	150
1880	150
1881	160
1882	160
1883	160
1884	190
1885	160
1886	290
1887	160
1888	160
1889	150
1891-O	185

Barber Quarters (1892–1916)
(Coins valued at $20 or more in average circulated condition)

1901-S Barber quarter. (Photo courtesy Auctions by Bowers and Merena, Inc.)

1892-S (with an S below the eagle)	20
1896-S	400
1897-S	20
1901-O (with an O below the eagle)	23
1901-S	1,350
1909-O	25
1913	30
1913-S	600
1914-S	25

Standing Liberty Quarters (1916–1930)
(Coins valued at $20 or more in
average circulated condition)

1916 Standing Liberty quarter, Mint State. (Photo courtesy Auctions by Bowers and Merena, Inc.)

1916	1,100
1917-D Type 1 (bare breast on Liberty and a D to the left of the date)	20
1917-D Type 2 (mailed breast on Liberty)	33
1917-S Type 2 (mailed breast on Liberty and an S to the left of the date)	26
1918-D	28
1918/17-S (with the 8 engraved over a 7)	1,100
1919	25
1919-D	85
1919-S	70
1920-D	30
1920-S	20
1921	100
1923-S	140

1924-D	30
1927-S	35

Washington Quarters (1932–present)
(Coins valued at $20 or more in average circulated condition)

1932-D (with a D below the eagle)	38
1932-S (with an S below the eagle)	26
1943-S doubled die (with doubling on the lettering on the front of the coin)	100
1950-D/S (with the D engraved over an S)	40
1950-S/D (with the S engraved over a D)	80

Flowing Hair Half Dollars (1794–1795)
(All dates are valuable)

1794	2,200
1795	500
1795 with three leaves under each wing of the eagle	2,200

Draped Bust/Small Eagle Half Dollars (1796–1797)
(All dates are valuable)

1796 with 15 stars on the front	15,000
1796 with 16 stars on the front	17,000
1797 with 15 stars on the front	18,500

Draped Bust/Heraldic Eagle Half Dollars (1801–1807)
(Coins valued at $500 or more in average circulated condition)

1801	500
1805/4 (with the 5 engraved over a 4)	550

Capped Bust Half Dollars (1807–1839)
(Coins valued at $100 or more in average circulated condition)

1807 with small stars on the front	150
1807 with large stars on the front	100

1812/1 large date (with the 2 engraved over a 1 and a large 8 in the date)	2,000
1815/2 (with the 5 engraved over a 2)	1,200
1836 with reeded edge and 50 CENTS	800

Seated Liberty Half Dollars (1839–1891)
(Coins valued at $100 or more in average circulated condition)

1840 with medium letters	175
1842-O small date (with an O below the eagle on the reverse)	1,200
1844-O doubled date	360
1846 with a horizontal 6	175
1846-O tall date	275
1847/6 (with the 7 engraved over a 6)	2,800
1850	250
1851	265
1855/54 (with the last 5 engraved over a 4)	140
1855-S with arrows beside the date and an S below the eagle	500
1857-S	100
1866-S without IN GOD WE TRUST	120
1870-CC (with the letters CC below the eagle)	1,100
1871-CC	200
1872-CC	100
1873-CC without arrows beside the date	200
1873-CC with arrows beside the date	200
1874-CC	400
1878-S	8,000

Barber Half Dollars (1892–1915)
(Coins valued at $50 or more in average circulated condition)

1892-O (with an O below the eagle)	150
1892-S (with an S below the eagle)	175
1894-O	50
1896-O	50
1896-S	75

1897-O	75
1897-S	90
1914	70

Walking Liberty Half Dollars (1916–1947)
*(Coins valued at $20 or more in
average circulated condition)*

1916	30
1916-D (with a D below IN GOD WE TRUST)	25
1916-S (with an S below IN GOD WE TRUST)	100
1917-D (with the D below IN GOD WE TRUST)	26
1917-S (with the S below IN GOD WE TRUST)	30
1919	25
1919-D (with a D on the reverse, above and to the left of HALF DOLLAR)	26
1919-S (with an S on the reverse, above and to the left of HALF DOLLAR)	20
1920-D (with the D on the reverse)	20
1921	150
1921-D (with the D on the reverse)	175
1921-S (with the S on the reverse)	50
1938-D (with the D on the reverse)	20

Flowing Hair Silver Dollars (1794–1795)
(Both dates are valuable)

1794	8,000
1795, type of 1794	1,000

Draped Bust/Small Eagle Silver Dollars (1795–1798)
(All dates are valuable)

1795	1,000
1796	1,000
1797 with 9 stars left, 7 stars right, and small letters	2,000
1797 with 9 stars left, 7 stars right, and large letters	800
1797 with 10 stars left, 6 stars right	800
1798 with 13 stars	1,200
1798 with 15 stars	1,800

Draped Bust/Heraldic Eagle Silver Dollars (1798–1804)
(All dates from 1798 to 1803 are valued at approximately $500 in average circulated condition; the 1804 is a great rarity worth upwards of $100,000 in average condition)

Gobrecht Silver Dollars (1836–1839)
(Coins valued at $1,000 or more in average circulated condition)

1836	1,800
1836 with new, slightly reduced weight	1,900
1839	2,000

Seated Liberty Silver Dollars (1840–1873)
(Coins valued at $500 or more in average circulated condition)

1850	500
1854	875
1855	800
1861	500
1870-S (7 to 12 known; an S below the eagle)	40,000
1871-CC (with the letters CC below the eagle)	2,650
1872-CC	1,200
1873-CC	3,500

Trade Dollars (1873–1885)
(Coins valued at $100 or more in average circulated condition)

1878-CC Trade dollar, Mint State. (Photo courtesy Auctions by Bowers and Merena, Inc.)

1873	100
1873-CC (with the CC mint mark above the D of DOLLAR on the reverse)	105
1873-S (with an S above the D of DOLLAR on the reverse)	100
1874	100
1875	250
1875-S/CC (with the S mint mark engraved over the letters CC)	200
1877-CC	140
1878-CC	385

Morgan Silver Dollars (1878–1921)
(Coins valued at $25 or more in average circulated condition)

1881-S Morgan dollar, Mint State. (Photo courtesy Auctions by Bowers and Merena, Inc.)

1879-CC (with the letters CC below the wreath)	32
1879-CC with a large CC engraved over a small CC	30
1880-CC with the reverse of 1878	30
1880-CC	28
1881-CC	60
1883-CC	25
1884-CC	58
1889-CC	150
1890-CC	25
1891-CC	25

1892-CC	28
1893	29
1893-CC	40
1893-O (with an O below the wreath)	40
1893-S (with an S below the wreath)	700
1894	150
1895-O	35
1895-S	60
1903-O	135

Peace Dollars (1921–1935)
(Coins valued at $25 or more in average circulated condition)

1921	25
1928	70

GOLD COINS

All gold coins have significant value because gold itself is so valuable. As this is written, the price of gold is approximately $400 per ounce. Since the largest regular-issue U.S. gold coin—the double eagle (or $20 gold piece)—contains very close to an ounce of gold, each and every example of this coin is worth several hundred dollars just as metal. Smaller gold coins are worth proportionally less as bullion, but even very small ones have respectable metal value. Many gold coins are worth a great deal more as collectibles, but the metal value of gold establishes a floor for even the commonest gold coins and those with substantial wear.

Following are values for some of the rarer and more collectible U.S. gold coins. As with all the previous coins in this compilation, the prices shown here are current retail values as of March 1996 for pieces in Fine-12, or average circulated condition.

Gold Dollars (1849–1889)
*(Coins valued at $1,000 or more in
average circulated condition)*

1855-D (with a D below the wreath on the reverse)	$ 1,200
1856-D with large head	2,000
1860-D	1,800
1861-D	3,800
1875	1,600

Capped Bust $2.50 Gold Pieces (1796–1807)
(All dates are valuable)

1796 with no stars	8,000
1796 with stars	7,800
1797	7,000
1798	2,600
1802/1 (with the 2 engraved over a 1)	2,450
1804 with 14 stars	2,600
1804 with 13 stars	12,000
1805	2,200
1806/4 (with the 6 engraved over a 4)	2,700
1806/5 (with the 6 engraved over a 5)	4,000
1807	2,200

Capped Draped Bust $2.50 Gold Pieces (1808)

1808	7,800

Capped Head $2.50 Gold Pieces (1821–1834)
(All dates are valuable)

1821	3,000
1824/1 (with the 4 engraved over a 1)	3,000
1825	3,000
1826	3,000
1827	3,000
1829 struck on a small planchet, or coin blank	2,600
1830	2,600
1831	2,800

1832	2,600
1833	2,500
1834	5,250

Coronet $2.50 Gold Pieces (1840–1907)
(Coins valued at $1,000 or more in
average circulated condition)

1854-D (with a D below the eagle on the reverse)	1,000
1854-S (with an S below the eagle on the reverse)	20,000
1855-D	1,500
1856-D	2,800

Three-Dollar Gold Pieces (1854–1889)
(Coins valued at $1,000 or more in
average circulated condition)

1854-D three-dollar gold piece. (Photo courtesy Auctions by
Bowers and Merena, Inc.)

1854-D (with a D below the wreath on the reverse)	5,000
1870-S (with an S below the wreath)	500,000
1873 with a closed 3	2,000

Capped Bust/Small Eagle $5 Gold Pieces (1795–1798)
(All dates are valuable)

1797 with 16 stars Capped Bust/small eagle $5 gold piece. (Photo courtesy Auctions by Bowers and Merena, Inc.)

1795	5,000
1796/5 (with the 6 engraved over a 5)	5,600
1797 with 15 stars	8,000
1797 with 16 stars	7,000
1798	16,000

Capped Bust/Heraldic Eagle $5 Gold Pieces (1795–1807)
(Coins valued at $2,500 or more in average circulated condition)

1797/5 (with the final 7 engraved over a 5)	4,000
1797 with 16 stars	5,000

Capped Head $5 Gold Pieces (1813–1834)
(Coins valued at $2,500 or more in average circulated condition)

1821	2,500
1825/1 (with the 5 engraved over a 1)	3,000
1826	2,600
1830 with small 5 D.	2,800
1830 with large 5 D.	3,000
1831 with small 5 D.	3,100
1831 with large 5 D.	3,200
1832 with square 2 and 13 stars	2,500
1833	2,600

1834 with plain 4	2,800
1834 with crosslet 4	2,900

Coronet $5 Gold Pieces (1839–1908)
*(Coins valued at $1,000 or more in
average circulated condition)*

*1864-S Coronet $5 gold piece, Mint State. (Photo courtesy
Auctions by Bowers and Merena, Inc.)*

1842-C small date (with a C below the eagle on the reverse)	1,200
1854-S (with an S below the eagle on the reverse)	10,000
1861-D (with a D below the eagle on the reverse)	2,500
1864-S	2,000
1870-CC (with the letters CC below the eagle on the reverse)	1,200
1878-CC	1,000

Capped Bust/Small Eagle $10 Gold Pieces (1795–1797)
(All dates are valuable)

1795 with 13 leaves	5,000
1795 with 9 leaves	15,000
1796	6,000
1797	6,800

Capped Bust/Heraldic Eagle $10 Gold Pieces (1797–1804)
(All dates are valuable)

1798/7 with 7 stars left, 6 stars right Capped Bust/heraldic eagle $10 gold piece. (Photo courtesy Auctions by Bowers and Merena, Inc.)

1797	2,500
1798/7 with 9 stars left, 4 stars right (with the 8 engraved over a 7)	6,500
1798/7 with 7 stars left, 6 stars right	12,500
1799	2,000
1800	2,650
1801	2,000
1803 with small stars	2,450
1803 with large stars	2,550
1804	3,250

Coronet $10 Gold Pieces (1838–1907)
(Coins valued at $1,000 or more in average circulated condition)

1870-CC Coronet $10 gold piece. (Photo courtesy Auctions by Bowers and Merena, Inc.)

1864-S (with an S below the eagle on the reverse)	2,500
1870-CC (with CC below the eagle)	1,250
1878-CC	1,000
1879-CC	1,800
1883-O (with an O below the eagle)	1,000

Liberty Head $20 Gold Pieces (1850–1907)
(Coins valued at $1,000 or more in average circulated condition)

1855-O (with an O below the eagle on the reverse)	2,000
1859-O	1,500
1860-O	1,850
1870-CC (with the letters CC below the eagle)	13,000
1871-CC	1,175
1879-O	2,000
1881	1,800
1885	1,200
1885-CC	1,000
1891-CC	1,050

Saint-Gaudens $20 Gold Pieces (1907–1933)
(Coins valued at $1,000 or more in average circulated condition)

1924 Saint-Gaudens $20 gold piece. (Photo courtesy Scott Travers Rare Coin Galleries, Inc.)

1907 with high relief, Roman numerals, and a wire rim	2,350

1907 with high relief, Roman numerals, and a flat rim	2,475
1920-S (with an S above the date)	2,500
1921	2,850
1927-D (with a D above the date)	6,000
1927-S	1,000
1929	1,000
1930-S	5,000
1931	4,800
1931-D	4,850
1932	5,000

PROOF SET PRICES

Proof sets aren't pocket-change rarities; in fact, they're not intended to circulate at all. These annual government sets of specimen-quality coins are normally acquired through purchase, rather than chance discovery. Nonetheless, they often turn up in old accumulations or in organized collections that someone in the family passes along. For that reason, I'm including them in this review of the fair market value of U.S. coins you're likely to encounter.

In recent years, late-date U.S. proof sets haven't kept pace with the rest of the coin market; their price performance hasn't been as spectacular as that of many other U.S. coins. This is not to say that proof sets aren't desirable; some are worth thousands of dollars—and almost all have great aesthetic appeal. However, for the most part, the beauty of these coins hasn't been matched by similarly beautiful escalation in value.

A generation ago, quite the opposite was true. Back in the 1950s and 1960s, many Americans made substantial profits every year by ordering proof sets from the Mint, then selling them to coin dealers for considerably more than what they had paid. At that time, the Mint was charging only $2.10 per set, and people who purchased these sets directly from the government were routinely able to sell them for 50 percent or 100 percent more than that—and sometimes even more.

In 1968, the Mint raised the price to $5 per set. To help justify this very sizable increase, it also introduced an attractive—but bulky—new holder. Up to then, the Mint had packaged proof sets in slender Pliofilm sleeves just about the size of a small letter-size envelope; in fact, it had mailed each set in an envelope just that size.

The new kind of holder introduced in 1968 offered greater protection for the coins; it was made of hard plastic that not only enhanced security but also was suitable for use in displaying the set. However, many people found this packaging inconvenient, since it took up so much space and thus made storage more difficult.

With this bulky plastic holder, people had three options:

1. They could display their proof sets around the house in these beautiful new holders.
2. They could store these bulky holders in their safety deposit boxes. But it didn't take many sets to fill an entire box, and safety deposit space was becoming more expensive.
3. They could put their rare coin investment dollars into other areas and forget about buying new proof sets every year.

Many people chose Option 3, reducing demand for new sets. Demand was further weakened by subsequent price increases. As this is written, the Mint is charging $12.50

apiece for new proof sets—nearly six times the issue price of pre-1965 sets—and unlike those, the standard sets today contain no silver coins. The Mint does offer silver sets as an option, but those now cost $21 each.

With all this in mind, it's really not advisable to spend much money today buying proof sets from the Mint. Your best bet is to order just one set every year, or only as many sets as you need for your own collection and for gift-giving.

If you're buying coins for investment, you're better off with other kinds of coins that appear to have greater potential for appreciation. Many of the proof sets made in recent years are available today for less than the Mint's original issue price. These sets really haven't recovered from the setback the market suffered when the government raised the price and introduced the hard plastic holders.

Many of the scarce and rare coins listed earlier in this chapter would be well worth keeping, rather than selling, if you found them. These coins have excellent prospects for going up in value even more—so if you don't need the money right now, it could be well worthwhile to hold them as investments. With proof sets, on the other hand, you should seriously consider selling any extras you may have, or any that you may find in a stash or a collection that comes your way.

Proofs are certainly beautiful to behold—but the later ones, at least, aren't likely to add any similar luster to your bank account. If some of the sets you're holding have sentimental value, by all means hang on to them. Just remember that while they may be worth a million dollars in a sentimental sense, their actual value is almost surely a great deal less than that—and it probably isn't rising very fast.

The U.S. Mint began making proof coins in the early nineteenth century; some U.S. coins produced even earlier are regarded as proofs by coinage experts. Sale of these coins to the general public began in the 1850s and—with occasional interruptions—has continued ever since.

The following list, however, is limited to proof sets produced by the U.S. Mint since 1936. These are the ones you're most likely to encounter in family collections or old accumulations you may find. Proofs made prior to 1936 all have significant value unless they are impaired in some way.

Proof Sets

1936	3,500
1937	2,000
1938	1,200
1939	1,000
1940	900
1941	600
1942	600
1942 Type 2	700
1950	500
1951	325
1952	200
1953	125
1954	65
1955	60
1955 flat pack	65
1956	35
1957	15
1958	25
1959	18
1960	15
1960 small date	20
1961	12
1962	12

1963	12
1964	11
1968-S	7
1968-S with no-S dime	8,500
1969-S	7
1970-S	9
1970-S small date	55
1970-S with no-S dime	400
1971-S	5
1971-S with no-S nickel	700
1972-S	5
1973-S	10
1974-S	10
1975-S	8
1975-S with no-S dime	28,000
1976-S three-piece 40-percent silver set	15
1976-S regular six-piece copper-nickel set	9
1977-S	10
1978-S	8
1979-S	9.75
1979-S Type 2	65
1980-S	8
1981-S	8
1981-S Type 2	300
1982-S	6
1983-S	8
1983-S with no-S dime	400
1983-S prestige set	80
1984-S	20
1984-S prestige set	50
1985-S	10
1986-S	25
1986-S prestige set	35
1987-S	8
1987-S prestige set	25
1988-S	15
1988-S prestige set	60
1989-S	10
1989-S prestige set	60

1990-S	13
1990-S with no-S cent	1,600
1990-S prestige set	50
1991-S	12.50
1991-S prestige set	70
1992-S	15
1992-S prestige set	60
1992-S silver	25
1992-S silver premier set	40
1993-S	15
1993-S prestige set	60
1993-S silver	20
1993-S silver premier set	39
1994-S	15
1994-S prestige set	60
1994-S silver	20
1994-S silver premier set	30
1995-S	15
1995-S prestige set	39
1995-S silver	20
1995-S silver premier set	39

PROOF COINS

There are also a number of individual proof coins with mint errors that can add considerably to their value. Here are some to look for:

- The 1983 no-S proof Roosevelt dime.

    I mentioned this variety earlier in the chapter. It won't turn up in pocket change, but if you or someone you know has any 1983 proof sets, take a close look at the dime. The mint mark was missing on some proof dimes that year, and these coins are worth up to $350.
- The 1974-S proof quarter with a double S.

The S mint mark on this coin has obvious doubling. Look for the S on the obverse (or "heads" side) of the coin, just behind Washington's pigtail.

• The 1973-S silver-clad proof Eisenhower dollar.

Most Eisenhower dollars are made from a copper-nickel alloy, rather than silver. But from 1971 to 1976, the Mint did produce special "Ike" dollars with limited silver content (40 percent, versus 90 percent in "traditional" silver dollars). These were made in both proof and uncirculated (business-strike) versions.

Of all the "silver Ikes," the scarcest and most valuable is the proof version minted in 1973. Only about a million of these were made—not very many, by modern minting standards—and, at one point, these were worth nearly $150 apiece, or 15 times their $10 issue price.

Strictly speaking, this isn't a "pocket-change rarity." Like all proofs, it's unlikely to turn up in ordinary change. Still, there's an excellent chance that you, or someone you know, may find one stuck away in a desk or cabinet. If so, you have a coin worth upwards of $30—and with the potential to rise in value substantially.

• The 1979-S clear-S Anthony dollar.

If you were around in 1979, you certainly remember the hullabaloo surrounding the Susan B. Anthony dollar. This "mini-dollar" coin—considerably smaller than its predecessors—was supposed to save the government enormous sums of money. In fact, it was intended as a permanent replacement for the $1 bill. The theory was that while this coin was somewhat more expensive to produce than a paper dollar, it would last many times longer, so production costs would be sharply curtailed in the long run.

The only problem was, people disliked the coin and

refused to use it. Many complained that because it wasn't much bigger than a 25-cent piece, they confused the new coin with the quarter and made expensive mistakes. In 1981, the Mint conceded defeat and suspended further production of Anthony dollars. But, by then, more than 800 million examples had been produced.

The public may have hated the coin, but hobbyists fell in love with at least one Anthony dollar: the "clear-S" or "Type 2" version of 1979.

Like most proof coins made by the U.S. Mint since 1968, Anthony dollar proofs were produced in San Francisco (with an "S" on the obverse just above Susan B. Anthony's right shoulder). On most proof dollars of 1979, the "S" looks like a blob. On some, however, the mint mark is clear and sharp. Being relatively scarce, these "clear-S" coins command a premium. The Type 1 proof set of 1979 (with a clogged "S" mint mark) costs about $10 at this writing, while the Type 2 set brings $65. All six coins in the set (the cent, nickel, dime, quarter, half dollar, and dollar) are either clear or clogged, as a rule, but the dollar is easily the most valuable. So check those desk and dresser drawers today!

HOLDING AND HOUSING YOUR COINS

It's very important to hold your coins properly. If you don't, they may suffer damage that will seriously compromise their value.

By now, perhaps you've gathered together a number of coins that you would like to set aside and store safely. Here, then, are some tips on how to care for your coins.

Always hold a coin tightly by the edges between your thumb and forefinger. Never take a finger and rub it over a coin; if you do, you may leave a mark that cannot be removed and will lower the coin's value significantly. Your hand contains natural oils which can cause irreparable damage to a Mint State coin (one that's in brand new condition), even reducing the grade of that coin from Mint State to lightly circulated. A single fingerprint across the face of a coin can decrease its value by tens of thousands of dollars.

You owe it to future generations of collectors to preserve your coins in the same condition you found them. What's more, you owe it to yourself: If you *don't* take care of your coins, you stand to lose a great deal of money when you sell them.

Proper storage of coins is also extremely important. Many people house their coins in folders, albums, or 2-by-2 cardboard holders. Doing so is better than not using any holder at all, and may be perfectly adequate for circulated coins. But these holders may not be good enough for coins in mint condition—those that have never passed from hand to hand.

Many coin albums have acetate inserts that are meant to protect the coins but which, in fact, can *harm* the coins when these inserts are pulled out or put back in. In sliding over the surfaces of Mint State coins, they can impart scratches or cause minute wear on the highest points. This kind of damage can never be repaired.

CLEANING AND POLISHING COINS

In general, you should never clean your coins. However, there's a difference between abrasive cleaning, where you penetrate the metal of the coin, and nonabrasive cleaning, which is restorative. Abrasive cleaning can ruin a coin's collectibility and destroy its premium value. But experts often use nonabrasive cleaning to restore a coin. For example, if a coin has a small piece of gum stuck to it, removal of the gum without penetrating the metal of the coin is deemed to be a restorative process.

Valuable coins should never be polished. Polishing a coin means cleaning it abrasively, and in doing so you remove the top layer of metal from the coin. That, in turn, removes details of the design from the surface—details which the designer and the Mint intended the coin to have when it was manufactured. By removing this detail, which can never be restored, you actually lower the grade of the coin.

There's also another problem: When you clean a coin abrasively, you penetrate its surface and activate the metal from which the coin is made. That sets in motion chemical reactions which often leave the coin far more unattractive than it was before you cleaned it, sometimes leaving the coin with unsightly blotches.

Before being placed in long-term storage, coins are frequently degreased using denatured alcohol. This helps protect them against unwanted chemical reactions that otherwise might occur with impurities in the environment. The alcohol doesn't damage the coins and doesn't penetrate their surface. But even the use of denatured alcohol should be left to the experts. And, if you use it, you should do so in a well-ventilated area.

STORING YOUR COINS

Coins should be stored in airtight containers, away from freely circulating air. Airborne particulate matter—particles you can't see—can lower a coin's value significantly.

Coins should also be stored in a stable environment, where the temperature is relatively moderate and constant. And if possible, they should be stored in the presence of a vapor-phase inhibitor—a chemical that changes the molecular composition of the surrounding air to help keep the coins from deteriorating due to environmental factors. A corrosion inhibitor marketed under the brand name Metal Safe is available from E&T Cointainer Company, P.O. Box 103, Sidney, OH 45365.

Coins should be stored in a dry environment. If you store your coins in a safety deposit box at your local bank, check to make sure that the bank doesn't have an ozone-purification or air-control system that regularly humidifies the air. Moisture is the enemy of coin preservation. From this standpoint, no-frills banks are often better repositories for rare coin collections, since they're less likely to have such elaborate air-purification devices.

The banks that have such systems are looking out for the interests of people who store documents in their safety deposit boxes. When paper gets dry, it turns yellow—so moisturizing the air helps preserve such documents. But as far as coins are concerned, dry and stable air is the perfect environment.

Speaking of paper, coins should be kept away from direct contact with paper. Paper contains sulfur, and sulfur causes coins to tarnish.

Take care of your coins and they will retain their beauty, and their value, for many years to come.

TONING OR CORROSION?

Some experts have questioned whether toning is merely a form of corrosion which can be likened to rust on a car. The process that causes silver coins to tone or tarnish, however, is different from the one that causes iron to rust.

My father, Harvey C. Travers, is a chemical engineer with a master's degree from the Massachusetts Institute of Technology, and he has carried out extensive studies on this subject. Some of his opinions are:

- When moisture reacts with iron, there is *an all-out destructive attack*—corrosion—of the metal. Iron spalls or loses metal when it rusts.
- Silver is relatively inactive and does not react with oxygen in the air, even at high temperatures. It reacts with certain chemical compounds, notably those containing sulfur, if a catalyst is present—moisture, for example. The reaction, however, stops short of being an all-out destructive attack. In the case of silver coins, the sulfur causes a protective coating to form on the surface of the metal.
- When silver tones or tarnishes, it is not eaten away—corroded—by this limited chemical reaction, and there is no loss of metal.

CHAPTER 4

ANSWERS TO THE MOST-ASKED COIN QUESTIONS

I'm called upon frequently to discuss rare coins on television talk shows and radio call-in programs. During these appearances, I get a lot of questions from the hosts of these shows, members of the studio audience, and viewers and listeners around the country.

Many of these questions come up again and again. This suggests to me that many of the people reading this book may have the same interests and concerns.

Here, then, are the questions most frequently asked of me, plus my answers.

What's the most valuable United States coin?

In October 1993, a 1913 Liberty Head nickel changed hands at a New York City auction for $962,500. That figure included a hammer price of $875,000 plus a 10 percent buyer's fee of $87,500. As of this writing, in March 1996, that stands as the highest price ever paid at auction—and the highest price confirmed to have been paid publicly—for a single United States coin. The coin was sold by Stack's of New York, a long-established numismatic auction house, on behalf of Reed Hawn, a prominent Texas collector who had purchased it in 1985 for $385,000.

In February 1996, the U.S. Secret Service aborted a pending sale which reportedly would have involved the expenditure of $1.5 million for a single U.S. gold coin. It did so by confiscating the coin—a 1933 Saint-Gaudens double eagle (or $20 gold piece)—on the grounds that double eagles never were officially issued by the government in 1933 and therefore are "stolen" and, thus, illegal to possess. The two dealers who reportedly had planned to broker the coin were arrested; as this is written, a defense is being mounted—and as part of that, the dealers could argue that 1993 double eagles were, in fact, issued by the government. It is documented that 445,500 of the coins were struck at the Philadelphia Mint, presumably in the full expectation that they would be released to circulation. However, virtually all of them were still in the government's hands when President Franklin D. Roosevelt issued his executive order recalling gold coins from circulation, and it is presumed that they were melted.

Ironically, the 1913 Liberty Head nickel has much more clouded origins than the 1933 double eagle, and yet has not been subject to seizure by the government. The Mint halted production of Liberty nickels at the end of 1912, with plans to begin the Buffalo nickel series in 1913. However, a handful of 1913 Liberty nickels turned up a few years later; five examples—all proofs—have been accounted for over the years. It's widely believed that these coins were produced surreptitiously—and probably illegally—by a Mint employee, using dies that had been prepared as a contingency. By contrast, no one disputes that the 1933 double eagles were officially struck by the Mint.

*I have a collection of medallions struck by The Franklin
Mint. They're attractive silver pieces portraying various
United States presidents. I understand that very few were
struck, and I have certificates from The Franklin Mint
which guarantee they're made of sterling silver.
Are these medallions valuable?*

Chances are, the items you have are worth no more than
"melt value"—the value of the silver they contain. Thousands of Franklin Mint issues were struck and sold for
substantial premiums, but a significant resale market never
materialized. Your "medallions" may be beautiful, but
they're not negotiable; you can't spend them. And since
there isn't a strong secondary market for these pieces as
collectibles, the only real value they have is their precious metal.

Remember, three factors determine the value of a coin
or medallion: (1) the level of preservation, which these
medallions probably have in their favor because they are
undoubtedly well preserved; (2) the number struck, and
many Franklin Mint items have relatively low mintages;
and (3) the collector base.

*I visited several countries in Europe a few years ago and
picked up coins everywhere I went during my travels.
Are they worth anything?*

Probably not. These coins are probably worth no more
than their face value in the countries where you obtained
them. Even if by chance you got some unusual variety, it
still isn't likely that these coins would command much
of a premium. There's simply not much of a market for
modern foreign coins.

The rare coin market in the United States is an easy-entry, easy-exit field; there is little regulation governing sellers of coins. Consequently, many of the people dealing in coins in this country are freewheeling entrepreneurs who don't have extensive backgrounds in areas of numismatics that are, quite literally, foreign. Most of these people don't speak foreign languages and don't really know much about foreign coins. They stick with the subject they're comfortable with—United States coins. Similarly, the overwhelming majority of coin collectors and coin investors in this country limit their purchases to U.S. issues.

Modern foreign coins do turn up in coin shops and at coin shows—but often they're in boxes containing common material that dealers sell by the pound for nominal sums. The foreign coins you acquired in your travels might very well be found in such a box.

My grandmother left me an old Buffalo nickel,
but I can't see the date. Is it worth anything,
and is there any way to restore the date?

That Buffalo nickel could be worth a million dollars—in sentimental value. But if you try to cash that in, you won't get more than a nickel.

Dateless Buffalo nickels are so worn that they're barely identifiable as to type. These coins don't have any collector value. Chemical date restorers are available—but while these might enable you to determine the date of the coin, they won't do a thing to enhance its collector value.

I just received a telephone call from someone I've never heard of, trying to sell me rare coins. What should I do?

Hang up the phone! Selling coins over the telephone is never a cost-effective proposition. Consequently, just about anyone who sells coins over the phone—via telemarketing—marks up their prices tremendously, in some cases several hundred percent. I'm sure there must be reputable telemarketers somewhere, but they're few and far between.

I've heard chilling horror stories about the abuses perpetrated by telemarketers. However, these go far beyond the scope of this response. Suffice it to say that if you're ever called on the phone by someone selling coins, someone you don't know, you should hang up the phone. Don't be polite. And never, under any circumstances, give your credit-card number over the telephone to someone that you have not called.

I talked to a coin-collector friend about selling some mint errors I found in change, but my friend said the coins I found weren't really "errors." Is he right?

There are many coins that deviate from the norm. Some are off-center and others exhibit doubled letters, to cite a couple. These coins were once lumped together as "mint errors." Now certain specialists argue that these coins should be classified under "minting varieties."

Author Alan Herbert is one of these experts. In Herbert's view, not every unusual coin is an "error." The coin may have been manufactured that way, perhaps because the mint was using worn dies to save money. Herbert differentiates between these *intentionally* different-looking coins and those that come out different *by mistake*. Only the latter, he argues, are really errors, but both come under the heading "minting varieties."

An excellent listing of minting varieties can be found in *Walter Breen's Complete Encyclopedia of U.S. and Colonial Coins* (Doubleday, 1988).

Last year, after reading a financial publication, I decided to invest $5,000 with a very good company that sells bullion and coins. I got several $20 gold pieces. They looked pretty and I put them away for a while. Last week, I decided to show them to a local coin dealer. He looked at them and said they're not worth anything. What should I do?

One thing you shouldn't do is accept the opinion of your local coin dealer without checking further. Any dealer to whom you bring coins for an appraisal has a vested interest in the outcome of the discussion. If you ask a dealer to render an opinion on coins that you purchased from a competitor, you really can't expect him to be objective. Human nature being what it is, that dealer isn't going to say: "You got a wonderful deal. You shouldn't buy coins from me; you should buy all your coins from my competitor." He's much more likely to say: "You got a terrible deal. These are horrible coins. You should return them and buy all your coins from me."

In buying coins and in getting coins appraised, you should always seek the protection of independent third-party grading. Buy only coins that have been certified by leading independent grading services. And before having coins appraised, submit them for certification by one of these firms. These organizations will encapsulate your coins in tamper-resistant, sonically sealed holders with inserts stating their grade. That way, you'll know what your coins are worth—or what they aren't worth.

I understand that coins are graded on a 1-through-70 scale. How can I tell the difference between a coin which grades 65 and is worth $5,000 and a similar coin which grades 64 and is worth only $1,000?

Don't expect to be able to tell the difference. Only trained experts can do this. But do apply a little common sense. If you have a portrait coin with a likeness of Miss Liberty, for example, look at the portrait. Her cheek is what is known as a grade-sensitive area. If you see nicks, marks, scratches, gouges, or other imperfections on that cheek, common sense should tell you that this particular coin probably won't qualify for a grade of Mint State-65.

There's a greater ethical burden on the coin dealer's shoulders than on someone who is selling a uniform commodity. Suppose you go out and buy yourself a television set—a brand-name 19-inch television set. As long as it comes in a factory-sealed box and has a U.S.A. warranty, you can be reasonably certain that you're getting what you're paying for. But if you buy coins which haven't been independently certified, you have no reasonable certainty as to what you're getting. If you don't know your coins, know your dealer. If you don't know either, get your coins independently certified. In fact, play it safe: Always get your coins certified by NGC, PCGS, or ANACS.

I've heard about independent certification, and I have some coins I might want to have certified. What certification services are reliable, and how do I get my coins certified by them?

As this is written, the three organizations which have the best reputations for strict, consistent grading—and whose coins therefore enjoy the greatest acceptance in sight-unseen trading—are the Professional Coin Grading Service (PCGS), the Numismatic Guaranty Corporation of America (NGC), and ANACS. Only ANACS accepts submissions directly from the general public. In the other two cases, you must take your coins to an authorized dealer member of the service whose certification you are seeking. The dealer will then submit the coins to the service on your behalf. (PCGS accepts coins directly from ANA members.)

You can write for a list of authorized PCGS and NGC dealers, or submit coins to ANACS, as follows:

Professional Coin Grading Service
P.O. Box 9458
Newport Beach, CA 92658

Numismatic Guaranty Corporation of America
P.O. Box 1776
Parsippany, NJ 07054

ANACS
P.O. Box 182141
Columbus, OH 43218-2141

> *I see that the price of common-date Mint State-65
> Morgan dollars is about $75 apiece. I saw an
> advertisement for coins that were independently
> certified as Mint State-65 by the Numismatic
> Certification Institute (NCI), and these were priced
> at $40 per coin. How can this be?*

The Numismatic Certification Institute (NCI) is a wholly owned subsidiary of Heritage Capital Corporation of Dallas, the world's largest rare coin dealer. As of this writing, NCI is not actively grading coins; however, many NCI-graded coins remain on the market. NCI standards—by Heritage's own admission—are from three-quarters of a point to a point-and-a-half more liberal than the standards set forth by NGC and PCGS. Thus, a coin graded Mint State-65 by NCI and priced at $50 might in actuality be the equivalent of only a Mint State-64 coin from either NGC or PCGS.

Whenever you buy coins, make certain you know which set of standards is being used to describe the coins' grade. There is no Santa Claus in numismatics—and if you're not careful, you could end up doing business with a Scrooge.

I found one of those 1989 Congress silver dollars with a rotated reverse. I told my local dealer that it's worth $600, and he thought I was nuts. Who would actually pay this price?

Anthony J. Swiatek, P.O. Box 218, Manhasset, NY 11030, says that he will pay $600 in cash as this book goes to press. However, this price is subject to change. Swiatek invites calls on the matter at 1-516-365-4120, and will take collect calls from people who have such coins to sell.

Where can I sell some of these other pocket-change rarities?

One of the leading market-makers in such material is Forman & Bauer Inc., 518 Ryers Ave., Bldg. 2, 1st Floor, Cheltenham, PA 19012. Forman & Bauer buys and sells just about any and all pocket-change rarities and pays very competitive prices. Be sure to call and confirm the arrangements first before sending any coins. The number is 1-215-663-1814.

*I'm a young collector and I don't have very much money,
but I'd like to get more involved in the hobby. I'd also
like to learn more about it. What should I do?*

The American Numismatic Association has set up a wonderful participatory educational program for young people. There's no charge to join or participate, and the program provides not only numismatic activities but also a social outlet. For further information, contact Lawrence J. Gentile Sr., 542 Webster Ave., New Rochelle, NY 10801, or call him at 1-914-632-5259.

Larry Gentile's programs include free seminars, free coins, free books, and a wealth of information that youngsters find helpful. To be placed on the Young Numismatist mailing list, you need only send to Larry a postcard with your name, address, and age. Please include your telephone number, as well.

*With certification of coins being so important, is there
any book I can buy that would explain in clear and
understandable terms exactly what standards are
used by these various certification organizations?*

There's an outstanding book entitled *How to Grade U.S. Coins*, by James L. Halperin. This book is published by Ivy Press Inc., a division of Heritage Capital Corporation, Heritage Plaza, Highland Park Village, Dallas, TX 75205, and costs $14.95 postpaid. The book contains color coin maps which walk you through the grading process. These will help you understand what's involved in the grading of coins and what factors each of the major grading services takes into consideration when assigning numerical grades.

*I have some silver dimes, quarters, and half dollars.
All of them are common-date coins, and all are well
worn from having circulated. I assume they're
worth just their bullion or metal value. How
can I determine what they're worth?*

The rule of thumb is that for every $1 of circulated silver
U.S. coins, the value is approximately 70 to 75 percent of
the price of a troy ounce of silver on that day. If you have
five silver dimes and one silver half dollar—or any other
combination adding up to $1—and the price of silver that
day is $4 an ounce, you'd probably be able to cash in
those coins for $2.80.

Of course, different equations are used for different coins.
The formula given here applies only to traditional U.S. silver coins with a silver content of 90 percent. These include
the dimes, quarters, and half dollars made before 1965.
Kennedy half dollars minted between 1965 and 1970 also
contain silver—but only 40 percent. You'll get less money
for these. Jefferson nickels made during World War II also
contain silver, but in an altogether different composition.

*I have about $500 to spend and I want to get involved
in buying coins. Where should I start?*

High-grade coins—those with grades of at least Mint
State-65 or Proof-65—performed very well in the market's last big boom—and although their prices have fallen
since then, they still hold great appeal. People want coins
in the very highest grades they can obtain, or at least in the
highest grades they can afford.

Demand in the coin market moves horizontally, not ver-
tically. If someone is collecting a certain kind of coin—
Morgan silver dollars, for example—in high Mint State
grades and the prices for these coins go up dramatically, that

buyer may find it difficult to purchase more Morgan dollars
in those grades. But rather than lowering his sights and buying Morgan dollars in lower grades, he'll probably turn
instead to a different kind of coin that's substantially less
expensive—and then collect that series in the same high
grades to which he was accustomed with Morgan dollars.

As this is written, one good starting place would be
Mint State-66 or Mint State-67 Mercury dimes. Another
would be Mint State-66 Walking Liberty half dollars. A
third would be Franklin half dollars graded Mint State-66
or even Mint State-67. All of these coins are affordable,
all of them have good potential, and all of them are quite
scarce in extremely high grades.

With Mercury dimes, for example, there are certain
dates for which only five or six specimens have been certified in Mint State-67. Yet some of these coins can be
purchased for less than $1,000—sometimes substantially
less—in Mint State-67. That's a tremendous value; you
really can't get hurt when you buy a coin like this.

Is there any one coin that you recommend
as the best to buy?

My favorite United States coin of all time is the Liberty
Seated quarter. Buy the highest grade you can afford. I
like both proof and business-strike examples (the coins
the Mint intended people to spend) in grades 65 and above
on the 1-through-70 grading scale. Different styles or
"varieties" of Liberty Seated quarters were struck from
1838 through 1891.

A "type" coin is a representative example of a particular coin series, but not one of the rarest and most valuable
specimens from that series. Experienced collectors and
investors have found certain type coins to be the big-

gest winners. I extend my highest recommendation—in high grades only—to the following: Liberty Seated dimes, quarters, halves, and dollars; Barber dimes, quarters, and halves; Bust dimes, quarters, halves, and dollars; Trade dollars; and nonmodern proof gold coinage. These coins are the blue chips, not the "sleepers," and have formed the backbone of the market for U.S. coins. But most importantly, these coins are beautiful.

How much can a dealer mark up coins sold for investment without getting in trouble with the government?

If you're selling something that's not an investment, you can charge whatever the market will bear. For example, if you buy a painting for $500 and sell it for $50,000, that's not illegal in itself. But if you represent that painting as a good investment, you'll surely have the watchdogs from the Federal Trade Commission sniffing down your neck, because the market value of that painting would have to go up spectacularly in a relatively short time to come even close to the $50,000 that your buyer was foolish enough to pay for it.

Barry J. Cutler, former director of the FTC's Bureau of Consumer Protection, says that when he was working for the commission, dealers selling items for investment tended to invite government scrutiny when they exceeded a markup of 100 percent, but that a 50-percent or even 75-percent markup (though this can be pushing it, he says) usually would escape the FTC's scrutiny. This doesn't mean that in private litigation in a civil court, a judge is going to give a dealer his or her blessing for a 75-percent markup—but based on the FTC's apparent yardstick, a dealer charging 50 percent or even 75 percent is probably free and clear.

Dealer representations can be very important in this area. Often, a dealer will claim to be charging a commission of only 2 or 3 percent when in fact he or she is charging 50 percent—in which case that person is committing fraud. By the way, Barry Cutler is now an attorney at McCutcheon, Doyle, Brown, and Enersen in Washington, D.C.

Why do I sometimes have to pay a lot more than the price-guide price for certain coins?

Coin market analyst Maurice H. Rosen of Plainview, New York, editor and publisher of the prize-winning *Rosen Numismatic Advisory*, several years ago came up with the term "market premium factor," or MPF to cover such situations. When you're purchasing coins, MPF refers to the percentage you're sometimes required to pay above published price-guide values.

Price guides are reflective of the marketplace, but the marketplace is not necessarily reflective of price guides. If a price guide says a coin is worth $1,000, but that coin is booming in the marketplace, suddenly you might have to pay $1,400, $1,500 or $1,600 to acquire it, even though the previous week's price guide indicated a market value of $1,000. So if you're at a coin convention and there's a particular coin you want, and the market for that coin is hot, just because your week-old pocket price guide says it's worth $1,000 doesn't mean you can write out a check for $1,000 to any dealer who has that coin and walk away with it.

If the market is hot, you need to use your intuition— your "market smarts"—in deciding what would be a fair market price for that coin. If the market is really booming, you might even have to pay upwards of $2,000 for that sought-after numismatic treasure.

CHAPTER 5

MARKETPLACE PSYCHOLOGY

To buy and sell coins advantageously, you need to understand what makes the market tick.

People who buy and sell coins are really no different from buyers and sellers in most other fields. They base their decisions on a number of different factors, both practical and emotional—and marketplace psychology plays an important part in determining what they buy or sell, and when they buy or sell it.

I've developed a three-step system to help you understand the psychology of the coin market—three easy steps by which you can determine how hot (or how cold) the coin investment environment may be at a given time by using the thermometer of market psychology.

These three basic steps are as follows:

- First, identify the prevailing psychological trend.
- Second, learn how *you* can benefit.
- Third, determine the proper way to buy and sell in this environment, taking into consideration the types of people you're dealing with and how much *more* than the price-guide price—or how much *less*—you'll have to pay when buying, or have to take when selling.

First, let's consider the question of psychological trends.

In the coin market as in many other markets, including the stock market, herd mentality governs most people's behavior. People feel very uncomfortable doing something alone.

People have a tendency to do things which are socially acceptable, and society encourages conformity. We can see this in the way young people are educated, not only in America but throughout the world. Conformity is encouraged; Those who are conformists are rewarded; those who are risk-takers are punished. Consequently, the vast majority of people do things to conform. They do things so they won't be viewed as outcasts.

This has quite a bit to do with psychological trends in the coin market. When the market has achieved a good deal of momentum and prices are higher than they've ever been before, this tendency to conform gives people a false sense of security. It makes them feel comfortable, and they continue to buy when, in actuality, they may very well be buying at the absolute height of the market.

Conversely, this predisposition to conformity makes people reluctant to buy when the market is weak. Since few other people are buying, they don't want to be non-conformist. Yet this may be the best time of all to buy. With the market at the bottom, there's very little "downside risk," as money experts like to call it—very little likelihood of losing money. In fact, there may be great "upside potential"—a strong possibility that prices will go up. But because of their reluctance to stand out from the crowd, many people won't take the plunge at such a time—even though the water may be perfect for investment.

Many of the world's greatest capitalists have been non-conformists—people who had no compunctions about deviating from the norm. These people have achieved remarkable success by disregarding the herd and following their own intuition—doing what their training and experience told them to do. They really haven't cared what was socially acceptable—or, for that matter, what they may have learned at some of our great institutions of learning. Keep in mind that even some of our finest business schools instill an overriding sense of conformity in their students. Thus, when they enter the marketplace, many graduates of these institutions—with all their knowledge and savvy—still find it difficult to buy when things seem bleak and others are sitting on the sidelines, even though their technical training would tell them to do otherwise.

In measuring the temperature of the marketplace, and thereby learning how to take full advantage of the thermometer of market psychology, you need to understand the distinction between a *bear* market and a *bull* market.

Whether in coins or any other field, a bear market is a period when people are selling things off—when the outlook seems grim and there isn't much hope on the horizon. In a bear market, you often see prices go down on a regular basis.

A bull market is just the opposite. People are extraordinarily enthusiastic—often falling all over each other in their headlong rush to buy coins.

In between a bull market and a bear market is a compromise situation called a *business-as-usual market*.

To simplify comparisons, let's calibrate our thermometer of market psychology from 1 to 10, with 1 being the coldest point and 10 being the hottest. (If you'd be more comfortable using some other type of scale, you're free to do so.)

On a 1-to-10 scale, it's prudent to sell when the market-place reaches a heat level of 8 or above, and it's prudent to buy at levels no higher than 6 or 7.

Let's say the market is gathering momentum; the increases have begun and the psychological level has moved up from 5 to 6. What you should do at this point is compare the current price of a given coin to its "book value"—how it has performed in the past—and try to determine where a reasonable person might expect it to go in the future. If the current price doesn't seem exaggerated by these standards, you can feel reasonably confident buying it, even at levels 6 or 7, with the goal of taking some short-term profits as it moves up from there toward 10.

Not too long ago, this type of thinking would have been looked upon as heresy. The conventional wisdom was to buy coins and hold them as long-term investments. The buy-and-hold philosophy isn't nearly as popular today. Experience has shown that it has some serious shortcomings, especially in regard to commoditized coins—those which change hands routinely on a sight-unseen basis like stocks and bonds. (We'll discuss these coins in greater detail in a later chapter.)

As part of your assessment of the market's overall temperature, you need to determine what's hot and what's not—what's the hottest area of the marketplace and what's the coldest.

You can trace the recent performance of various kinds of coins by following the price charts in major periodicals that cater to buyers and sellers in this field. Coins that are hot are probably showing phenomenal increases in these charts, possibly reflected by plus signs. Coins that are cold may have dropped in value sharply and may have minus signs. Keep in mind that very few coin advisory services recommend when to *sell* coins. Their emphasis is on *buying*. Thus, it is difficult to know when to sell unless you monitor market levels yourself.

Pricing information is featured regularly in all of the following publications, some of which are readily available on newsstands:

- The *Coin Dealer Newsletter*, P.O. Box 11099, Torrance, CA 90510 ($54 for 26 weekly issues, $98 for 52 issues, plus free monthly supplements). This publication, known as the "Greysheet," gives authoritative values for "raw" coins (those not certified by one of the grading services).

- The *Certified Coin Dealer Newsletter*, P.O. Box 11099, Torrance, CA 90510 ($65 for 26 weekly issues, $117 for 52 issues). This publication, known as the "Bluesheet," gives widely accepted values for certified coins.

- *Coin World*, P.O. Box 150, Sidney, OH 45365 ($28 per year in the United States; add $40 outside the U.S.; weekly newspaper). Prices are featured in the weekly Trends Value listings by Keith M. Zaner.

- *Numismatic News*, 700 East State Street, Iola, WI 54990 ($27.95 in the United States, $79.95 outside the U.S.; weekly newspaper). Prices are featured in the Coin Market listings by Bob Wilhite.

- *COINage*, 4880 Market Street, Ventura, CA 93003 ($23 per year in the United States; $32 outside the U.S.; monthly magazine). Price trends are shown in *The COINage Price Guide*.

- *Coins*, 700 East State Street, Iola, WI 54990 ($22.95 per year in the United States; $32.25 outside the U.S.; monthly magazine). Prices are featured in the Coin Value Guide, edited by Bob Wilhite.

COINage and *Coins* are both available on news-stands just about everywhere. To obtain the other publications, you may have to take out subscriptions.

In determining what's hot and what's not, you won't find every decision cut and dried. Sometimes, certain coins are just lukewarm. Other times, given items may remain out of favor for extended lengths of time, and thus may stay at the bottom, rather than moving up in a cyclical way. With this in mind, it's not a good idea to assume that just because something is cold, it's bound to turn warmer sometime soon.

THE THEORY OF MARKET CYCLES

One of the most respected experts in the coin field, professional numismatist Q. David Bowers of Wolfeboro, New Hampshire, has expounded a theory of market cycles. This theory can be applied to the marketplace as a whole or to just one specific type of coin.

Bowers contends that "each cycle seems to take place on a succeedingly higher plateau." Suppose the price of a given coin bottoms out at Point A, rises to a high at Point B, drops to another low at Point C, then rises again to a second high at Point D. Under Bowers' theory, Point C won't be as low as Point A, and Point D will be higher than Point B. Basically, such a scenario indicates a steady and growing marketplace.

This is sometimes true with *rare* coins—very low-mintage coins costing hundreds or thousands of dollars. However, we've seen some notable exceptions in the more commoditized items such as Morgan silver dollars, Peace dollars, and Walking Liberty half dollars. We saw lows in 1990 which were lower than the lows of five years earlier—and in some cases lower than the lows of *seven* years earlier. These coins are really not all that rare; some of them, in fact, are relatively common. At the time of this writing, there just aren't as many buyers as there are coins of some issues. As discussed in the previous chapter, these common coins often need economic justification (such as anticipation of inflation) for a value increase.

The theory is sound, but it doesn't work for every series and every situation, as Bowers himself concedes. If there is a variable which causes buyer disinterest, it might take two hundred years for a coin that's very cold to get very hot, and no one wants to base investment decisions on cycles that require two hundred years for a coin's new high to be higher than its previous high.

HEALTHY, GROWING MARKETS

One of the keys to making a solid purchase, in coins or in anything else, is to stick with an item that conforms to Q. David Bowers' theory of market cycles—in other words, an investment whose lows are higher than the previous lows, and whose highs are higher than the previous highs.

If we were to formulate a graph based upon a rare coin investment meeting these criteria, what we would see is a gradual but continuous upward line. This, in turn, would indicate a healthy, thriving, and growing area of the market. The theory of market cycles may be hypothetical, and may be better suited to a textbook than it is to the workaday world of buyers and sellers, but many coins do indeed enjoy steady upward movement, and this can be quite impressive when it is expressed in graphic form.

Consider Figure 1, for example. This is a graphic depiction of the marketplace performance of Type 2 Indian Head gold dollars (U.S. $1 gold pieces minted from 1854 to 1856) in Mint State-65 condition. It covers the period from 1986 to 1990. The low value was $22,000; the high value was $46,700. And although there are many lows and many highs, and this coin's performance illustrates the new volatility of the rare coin marketplace, the general trend when we look at the graph is upward. These coins are climbing in value consistently—and in fact dramatically.

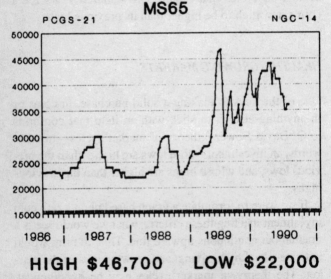

Figure 1. *Indian Head gold dollars, Type 2 (Graph courtesy of Richard Nachbar, c/o Jack Hunt-Coin Broker, P.O. Box 194-R, Kenmore, NY 14217)*

Figure 2 charts the market performance of Mint State-65 Trade dollars during the same period. (Trade dollars are large silver U.S. coins similar in size and shape to silver dollars, which were used in foreign commerce during the latter part of the nineteenth century.) From 1986 to 1990, the low value of these coins was $4,500 and the high was $22,000. And while the chart shows some spiked highs and volatile lows, the general trend is upward.

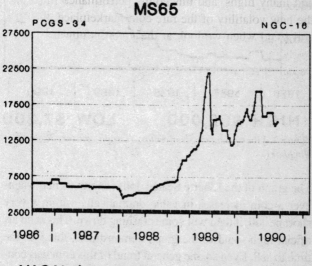

HIGH $22,000   LOW $4,500

Figure 2. *Trade dollars (Graph courtesy of Richard Nachbar)*

Figure 3 tracks the performance of Mint State-65 Liberty Seated silver dollars bearing the motto *IN GOD WE TRUST* (this motto appeared only during the final few years of the series). From 1986 to 1990, these coins moved between a low value of $7,300 and a high of $52,000—and, once again, the general trend was upward.

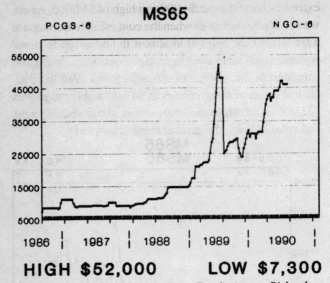

MS65

PCGS-6   NGC-6

HIGH $52,000   LOW $7,300

Figure 3. *Liberty Seated silver dollars (Graph courtesy Richard Nachbar)*

The graph of the Liberty Seated dollar shows us that whenever a coin increases in value dramatically within a very short period, it then will come crashing down. This is an artificial high—and as the graph demonstrates, this was the time to sell. Even so, the general trend of this coin was consistent, reassuring—and upward. The only exception is the time when it surged dramatically in a very short period, then fell right back. And, even then, after falling to that low, it gradually climbed again almost to the previous high.

Figure 4 depicts the upward movement of yet another coin that fits the Bowers theory of market cycles. This time, the coin is the Liberty Seated half dollar without the motto *IN GOD WE TRUST*, again in the grade of Mint State-65. Between 1986 and mid-1990, the market range of this coin extended from a low of $4,000 to a high of $17,000. Again, we see one time in 1989 when the coin escalated in value at a frenzying pace and fell to almost the point where it had been before. Thereafter, it climbed, but not quite to the high it experienced in 1989. But, in 1990, it still was considerably higher than it had been in 1986 and the overall growth pattern once more appeared consistent and reassuring.

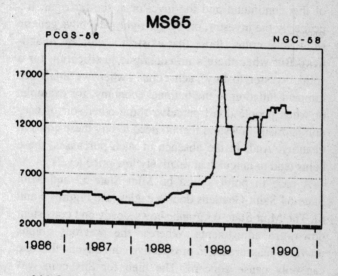

HIGH $17,000   LOW $4,000

Figure 4. *Liberty Seated half dollars, without the motto* IN GOD WE TRUST *(Graph courtesy Richard Nachbar)*

There are many coins like this. In fact, most rare coins had this reassuring upward pattern in years gone by. However, there are also some exceptions to this pattern of growth. Rather than moving consistently higher in value, some coins display a consistently *downward* trend. I've gone into considerable depth about some of these types of coins.

You can still make money trading these coins—but the trick is to *trade* them, not hold them over a long-term period. Over the long term, unless there's economic justification for these coins to increase in value, they're simply not going to perform all that well.

Let's go back to the continuum I wrote about in Chapter 1. As you may recall, I showed the collector at the left of this continuum and the investor at the far right. It's primarily the investor, on the far right, who buys generic Mint State coins (those that exist in significant quantities). But when there's no economic justification for a solid investor to buy such coins—when we don't see rampant inflation in the national economy, for example, or when people don't perceive some other sort of economic crisis, investors feel no need to buy these coins in quantity. And, in the absence of such purchases, these coins tend to languish at relatively low price levels.

A case in point would be Mint State-63 and Mint State-64 Saint-Gaudens double eagles (see Figures 5 and 6). The Mint State-63 graph shows steady and consistent downward adjustments. Whereas the previous graphs provided reassurance to prospective coin buyers, this one can only cause concern. The high for this coin was $1,280 and the low was $530—but the high occurred in 1986 and the low came in 1990, and the coin decreased in value consistently during the period. The Mint State-64 Saint-Gaudens double eagle fluctuated between a high of $2,400 in 1986 and a low of $810 in 1990, and again we see a steady downward trend. A major reason for this was the availability, since 1986, of American Eagle gold bullion coins, which bear the same design as the Saint-Gaudens double eagle on one side.

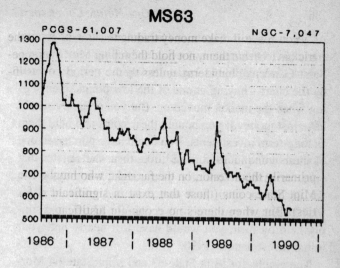

MS63

PCGS-51,007   NGC-7,047

HIGH $1,280   LOW $530

Figure 5. *Saint-Gaudens $20 gold pieces (Graph courtesy Richard Nachbar)*

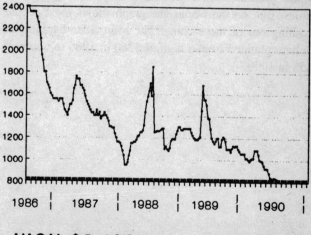

MS64

PCGS-27,283   NGC-5,848

HIGH $2,400   LOW $810

Figure 6. *Saint-Gaudens $20 gold pieces (Graph courtesy Richard Nachbar)*

As we can see in Figure 6, tremendous sums of money could have been made by buying and selling Mint State-64 Saint-Gaudens double eagles during the period covered by the chart—buying at one of the low points, then selling when the market moved up. But you certainly would have lost money if you bought these coins and held them as long-term investments. You could have purchased one of these coins in 1988 for $1,000, then sold it later that year for $1,800; similarly, you could have bought one for $1,200 in 1989, then turned around and sold it for $1,700. But, if you bought that coin for $1,000 and simply held on to it, you would have lost nearly half your initial investment by 1990.

The graphs for Mint State-63 and Mint State-64 Morgan dollars (Figures 7 and 8) are similar: consistently down. The Mint State-63 coins fell from a high of $100 in 1986 to a low of $28 in 1990. Again, there were rallies which presented some dramatic money-making opportunities. But, on the whole, the graph shows most people cashing out of these coins. The Mint State-64 Morgan dollars plunged from a high of $260 in 1986 to a low of $58 in 1990.

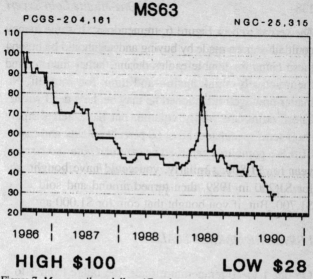

MS63

PCGS-204,161   NGC-25,315

HIGH $100   **LOW $28**

Figure 7. *Morgan silver dollars (Graph courtesy Richard Nachbar)*

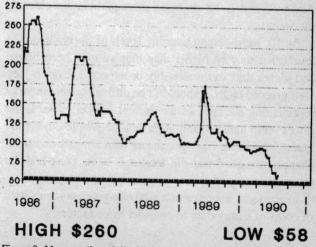

MS64

PCGS-211,761   NGC-39,549

HIGH $260   **LOW $58**

Figure 8. *Morgan silver dollars (Graph courtesy Richard Nachbar)*

The lesson to be learned is quite apparent: If some investment adviser comes to you and says you should be buying these coins for long-term investment, rather than trading them actively, think again—and think for yourself. No matter how well-intentioned he may be, he's dead wrong. These coins are wildly volatile, but have netted many short-term speculators 50 or 60 percent quickly and easily. This is a gambler's game, so be careful. *Under no circumstances should you buy these coins and hold them with the goal of gaining long-term appreciation.*

USING THE MARKET SCALE

On our 1-to-10 temperature scale, the range from 1 to 3 corresponds to a time when the coin market is quite cold and people are pessimistic about the outlook. By 4 and 5, the market is fundamentally healthy and getting stronger. And by 6 and 7, we see many more participants entering the arena.

By 10, we're seeing amazing levels of overvaluation—levels that may be higher than they've ever been before and higher than can reasonably be expected. Even if they aren't record highs, it shouldn't be difficult to spot them as representing the apex of the current market cycle. If the prices seem unreasonably high and the people buying the items seem more like speculators than shrewd investors, chances are good that the market is at its peak and the prices are going to decline very sharply and very soon.

In assessing the price potential of a given coin or series of coins, it's important to consider three factors:

- The grade of the coin—how well preserved it is and how many nicks, scratches, or other flaws it has on it.
- How many people collect that particular type of coin.
- The number of examples of that coin that are available.

If you see a coin, or a series of coins, that has tens of thousands of pieces available and it seems to be enjoying popularity at the moment, but it doesn't have a solid base of dedicated collectors, stay away from it. It's probably a fad, and its current market value is probably exaggerated.

We saw an example of this in the late 1980s—not with coins, but rather with a series of one-ounce silver medals bearing portraits of Walt Disney characters. Initially, these were offered at prices not much higher than the value of the silver they contained. Within a couple of months, as dealers promoted them, they were being sold for hundreds of dollars apiece. It was clear that there wasn't a very strong collector base for these medals; what's more, a single company controlled the number available—which, in relative terms, was rather high.

Predictably enough, this turned out to be a fad that died away. A lot of the values have dropped rather sharply, and as this is written the medals can be obtained for just a small fraction of their highs.

As this example illustrates, you really need to use your intuition and common sense and not simply follow the crowd.

Besides being able to identify the prevailing psychological trend, you should also have the ability at this point to judge the market objectively and rationally, standing at an arm's-length distance from the people in the arena who are either too excited or too pessimistic. *You* now know the market's tendencies and understand how coin buyers think and act. This should give you a tremendous advantage over the herd, and over buyers and sellers who are blindly and unthinkingly following that herd—if not to the slaughter, then at least to a substantial financial bath.

ROTATIONAL LEADERSHIP

Another factor you have to keep in mind in assessing the coin market's psychology is the issue of *rotational leadership*. This sounds like a complicated concept, but its meaning is really quite simple: In a rip-roaring bull market, different coins often take turns increasing in value.

One week, commemorative coins may jump in price. Another week, silver dollars may go up. The next week, the big winner may be Liberty Seated quarters or Barber half dollars. Some coins may level off while others are taking a turn. Thus, in a sense, the baton is passed around so that different kinds of coins lead the advances.

Rotational leadership also can occur in a marketplace retreat. In a declining marketplace, you might see silver dollars decreasing in value one week, type coins (representative coins of a particular series which are not rare dates of that series) might be the biggest losers the next week, and yet another series—commemoratives, perhaps— might then take a hit the week after that.

Rotational leadership should be taken into account when assessing the strength or weakness of any particular area of the market. Before deciding just how bullish or bearish Morgan silver dollars are, for example, you also need to look at other major areas of the market. Check your price guides to see how commemoratives or Walking Liberty half dollars are doing; while you're at it, take a look at type coins. The market is a mosaic, and every piece has bearing on every other one.

BENEFITING FROM MARKET PSYCHOLOGY

Now that you understand the thermometer of market psychology, you can learn very quickly and easily how to benefit from its use. This brings us to the second of our three basic steps in understanding and using marketplace psychology.

Before going any farther, it's worth recalling an old expression often heard on Wall Street, but equally true with rare coins: "Bulls make money, bears make money, but pigs lose out." Keep in mind, too, that there's a name for people who always buy low and sell high. They're called liars. Suffice it to say that one of the primary ways to benefit from market psychology is not to be a pig—not to try to squeeze every last dime out of every deal.

Let's say you've bought a coin at level 6 or level 7 on our market-cycle scale of 1 to 10. As the market then climbs closer to the top, you'll start to notice shudders—chinks in the market's armor, if you will. But, while there may be some small disappointments, the feeling will persist that there's no place to go but up. It's sort of like a boxing match where one of the boxers absorbs a couple of whacks but stays on his feet and seems to be going strong. Then comes the knockout punch—a 10-count for the boxer but a knockdown for the coin market all the way from 10 back to 1.

You have to be on your guard. A hot market is persuasive; it mesmerizes you and lures you in. The time to sell that coin you bought at level 6 is really level 7 or level 8;

if you wait for level 10, you'll probably end up owning it back at level 1.

Contrary to what you may have been told, the coin market is not a standard financial market. It's a supplement to traditional modes of investment. And, at the time of this writing, it's a totally unregulated marketplace, in no way subject to the jurisdiction of either the Securities and Exchange Commission (SEC) or the Commodity Futures Trading Commission (CFTC). The only government activity now taking place in this industry is the limited involvement of the Federal Trade Commission (FTC), which has charged a number of coin dealers with false, deceptive, and misleading practices in trade and in commerce. These dealers have signed consent decrees with the commission and this has served to clean up the industry.

Because of the absence of government controls, the coin market may react differently from standard financial markets. Thus, when the coin market shudders, prices may continue to escalate—go right through the stop sign, so to speak. In large part, that's because there isn't a federal "policeman" sitting behind a billboard at the corner. This is expected to change shortly.

Under the circumstances, you have to be able to recognize the stop signs and police your own buy-and-sell activities. Otherwise, you may end up being one of the victims when the market crashes.

For one thing, you should watch for signs of rotational leadership. If you see several different areas of the market experiencing declines in value in a relatively short period, the market may be sending you a signal: It may be saying the boom-and-bust theory is absolutely true and that bulls and bears make money while pigs—those who are too greedy—just make bacon and ham.

ACTUAL BUYING AND SELLING

The third and final step in understanding and using market psychology involves the actual buying and selling of coins.

For all practical purposes, you'll have to deal with a dealer in buying coins. Rare coins are viewed as a credence good. In other words, you—as a nondealer—are not expected to be able to tell the difference between a coin grading Mint State-64 and its counterpart grading Mint State-65. The burden is on the dealer or, in a sense, on the grading service whose product you are buying.

Leading coin-grading services have somewhat solved the grading problem for you. You don't have to know how to grade coins; you don't have to be able to tell the difference between a 65 and a 56. As I explained earlier, these expert services have achieved outstanding records for accuracy and consistency, and you can rely on their judgments. Nevertheless, still use your common sense. If a coin looks ugly to you, don't buy it.

What you *do* need to know about is pricing.

You can work out commissions with your dealer. But you should be aware that many dealers have earned commissions of 75 percent—or even 100 percent—and yet haven't been viewed as overcharging their clients. Substantial legal precedent exists on this point: The Federal Trade Commission, for example, has allowed some coin merchants to charge upwards of 90 percent as a commission or markup.

You're entitled to ask your dealer how much of a markup he's charging—and you should. And you should make every effort to limit this premium, especially when you're buying certified coins. Because of their liquidity, these normally carry much more modest markups than "raw" coins—those that haven't been certified.

In a very hot market, or even just a moderately hot market (one that might rate a 7 on the 1-to-10 scale), you'll probably have to pay a premium over the values published in the price guides.

Let's say prices are increasing at frequent intervals and let's say you're purchasing a Liberty Seated quarter whose wholesale price-guide value (the typical cost to a dealer) is $5,000. In order for a dealer to buy that coin in a rising market, chances are he'll have to pay $5,500 or $5,800. Newsletter writer Maurice Rosen calls this the "market premium factor." Obviously, the dealer will then have to charge *you* more, as well.

In a business-as-usual market (5 on the 1-to-10 thermometer) or a cold market (1, 2, 3, or 4), you can buy coins very close to the levels in the wholesale price guides. In fact, in such markets, dealers sometimes get nominal discounts off the wholesale prices. These discounts are not tremendous; they might amount to 3 to 5 percent. Still, they represent savings that the dealer can then pass along. In a rip-roaring bull market, by contrast, a dealer might have to pay 10 percent more than the level in current price guides.

This is really an anticipatory factor. It's based on what the market is expected to do in the very near future. If the market is in the 7 position, for example, you may have to pay $6,500 for that Liberty Seated quarter that shows up on the wholesale price list at $5,000. That's because with prices trending higher, short-term profits can be made, and these are being anticipated each time the coin changes hands.

Does this mean your dealer is pocketing a profit of

$1,500? Not necessarily. In fact, there's an excellent chance that he's making a good deal less—say, $500 or so.

There you have it: the way to understand the psychological makeup of the rare-coin marketplace and use the thermometer to your advantage.

The coin market, like the weather, can be changeable. At times, it can be as hot as the Sahara and at other times as cold as a barren tundra. But if you equip yourself with the tools in this chapter, you'll find that you can prosper in any kind of weather from 1 to 10.

CHAPTER 6

GRADING IN FIVE EASY STEPS

The value of a coin varies—often dramatically—in accordance with its "grade," or level of preservation. As a coin passes from hand to hand (or "circulates"), it becomes increasingly worn and loses detail which can never be regained. This, in turn, erodes its value as well. By determining the *grade* of a coin, you go far toward determining its *value*.

The grade assigned to a coin is really a kind of shorthand used by knowledgeable "numismatists," or coin collectors, to tell each other what the coin looks like. Many coins are purchased through the mail, and when buying in this manner it is helpful to know beforehand how they look. The grade used by the seller to describe such a coin, or assigned by a grading service, tells a great deal about the coin's appearance and thereby lets you gauge how much you should pay.

Numismatists use a 1-through-70 scale to communicate information regarding coins' level of preservation, or grade. The number assigned to each coin depends on a number of factors: how much wear it has suffered, how many scratches or nicks or dents or other imperfections it may have, and basically how appealing—or, for that matter, how *unappealing*—it may be.

The number 1 denotes a coin which is barely identifiable as to its type—a cent on which Abraham Lincoln's portrait is barely discernible, for example. At the other end of the grading spectrum, 70 denotes a coin which is perfect—one which has no nicks, no flaws, no scratches, and no imperfections of any kind.

In practice, the number 70 is rarely used. For all practical purposes, from the moment they are minted most coins have flaws which preclude their designation as "perfect."

The 11 numbers from 60 through 70 are set aside for "Mint State" coins—coins which have never entered circulation. A coin graded anywhere from 60 to 70 has never passed from hand to hand and thus has no friction on its high points. It is said to be "uncirculated."

Mint State coins are highly prized, and you should take great care of any coin you may possess which merits a grade from 60 to 70. The slightest touch from your fingers can lower the grade of a Mint State coin considerably. Suppose you owned a coin that was graded 65—Mint State-65—on a scale from 1 to 70. If you were to take your perspiration-soaked thumb and rub it over the coin, that single touch might lower the coin's value by several thousand dollars. That's why it's important to hold a coin only by its edge and never touch it directly on the front ("obverse") or back ("reverse").

For grading purposes, there are three basic categories of coins you need to know about. All three will be discussed in this chapter, and after you finish reading about them you will be much more expert at grading coins. It's all here, it's fun, it's easy—and, most important of all, once you've read this chapter and mastered its principles and lessons, you will find it to be extraordinarily profitable.

The first category you need to know about is *Mint State* coins. The second is *proofs*. And the third is *circulated* coins. Learn the grading principles involved with these three basic categories and you will master the process of coin grading—and with it coin pricing.

MINT STATE COINS

Coins which are "Mint State" have no friction on their very highest points, have not passed from hand to hand, and are not circulated.

Learning how to grade Mint State coins, or at least understand what numismatists look at when grading these coins, is vital to your success as a buyer or seller. The reason is basic economics: A coin graded Mint State-67 can be worth thousands of dollars—even tens of thousands of dollars—more than a similar coin graded Mint State-65.

No nonprofessional can be expected to master the grading of Mint State coins with 100-percent consistency. For that reason, it's important to have an independent grading service examine these coins for you. The three leading services as this is written are the Numismatic Guaranty Corporation of America (NGC), located in Parsippany, New Jersey, the Professional Coin Grading Service (PCGS) of Newport Beach, California, and ANACS of Columbus, Ohio.

Even professionals have to work long and hard to perfect their skills at grading Mint State coins. John Albanese, founder of NGC, has told me that it took him four years to be able to tell the difference consistently between Mint State coins grading 64 and Mint State coins grading 65.

The grading of Mint State coins is a five-step process; when you grade these coins, just say to yourself: "1-2-3-4-5." That will help you recall the five easy steps you need to consider: surfaces, luster, toning, strike, and eye appeal. Remember: "1-2-3-4-5 . . . surfaces, luster, toning, strike, and eye appeal."

SURFACES

When we speak about the "surfaces" of a coin as an element of grading, we're referring to the number of scratches, gouges, or other imperfections the coin may have. Even Mint State coins have such imperfections; however, the more they have, the lower their grade will be.

With rare coins as in few other fields, beauty is truly skin-deep, and the surfaces are of supreme importance.

Let's start by considering coins graded Mint State-65 (or MS-65). This is not the highest grade; in fact, it's in the exact center of the 60-to-70 Mint State grading range. But MS-65 is a benchmark grade—a point of reference used in determining other Mint State grades that are higher and lower. It's also at the top of the "normal" Mint State range; anything higher than Mint State-65 is viewed as a "supergrade" coin—one with exceptional appeal and a correspondingly exceptional price tag.

MS-65 coins can have a few scattered marks, but nothing too heavy or noticeable. A similar coin with a few additional marks, or with marks in more obvious locations, would probably be downgraded to MS-64 if all other factors were equal. Similarly, a coin with fewer marks might merit a grade of MS-66.

Mint State-60 (or MS-60) is another benchmark grade. MS-60 coins barely qualify as uncirculated; they are the least desirable of the Mint State coins. Generally speaking, an MS-60 coin is not especially attractive; it may have heavy bag marks, abrasions, or other imperfections and these may be easily discernible with the naked eye. On large coins such as silver dollars or $20 gold pieces, there may be an especially obvious gash or other mark in a high, exposed area of the design. Nonetheless, an MS-60 coin will betray no evidence of wear—or having passed from hand to hand—and thus will be technically uncirculated.

The final two benchmark grades within the Mint State range are Mint State-63 (or MS-63) and Mint State-67 (or MS-67). Like the other basic MS grades (MS-65 and MS-60), these serve as reference points for grades above and below them. One professional grader puts it this way: "These benchmark grades are the automatics; when a Mint State coin doesn't quite fit one of these four categories, you have to embellish and fill in the grades in between."

Coins graded MS-63 are seen at independent grading services more often than any other kind. These are attractive coins, but less so than those graded MS-65 and MS-64. They can—and probably do—have marks that attest to handling or possibly stacking. However, these marks must be light. They would be much less apparent than the surface imperfections on a coin graded MS-60.

MS-67 coins are truly premium pieces. They can have one or two very small detracting surface marks—"faint faults," as one grader puts it, but these must be visible only under a 5-power magnifying glass. Looking at an MS-67 coin, it's easy to see why collectors and investors alike find such coins so appealing and are willing to pay big premiums to obtain them.

Mint State-69 (or MS-69) coins are very nearly perfect. In practice, this is probably the highest grade you'll ever see assigned to a certified coin, since MS-70—the ultimate grade—has come to be regarded as all but unattainable.

Don't expect to see too many coins graded MS-69, either. A coin doesn't have to be perfect to merit this grade, but it has to be so close that very few coins pass the test. An MS-69 coin must have no visible imperfections, even under 10-power magnification. One or two rim flaws may appear, but they must be almost imperceptible even under the glass.

Mint State-68 (or MS-68) coins aren't far behind. These, too, look nearly perfect to the unaided eye and betray only very minor flaws under a 10-power glass.

MS-69 and MS-68 coins are "wonder coins" in the finest sense of the term. As one coin enthusiast I know comments: "They practically glow in the dark, they're so beautiful."

The number of scratches and other detracting marks visible on a Mint State coin are key indicators of its grade. A coin that looks as if a city bus ran over it, or looks as if your mother-in-law threw it out the window—a coin with nicks, marks, scratches, gouges, and other abrasions all over it—cannot be in a high grade, no matter what anyone says, even if that someone is a coin-grading service. So use your common sense when you look at any coin. If it's nicked, marked, gouged, or severely dented, don't buy the coin, no matter what any dealer or grading service says.

LUSTER

In our 1-2-3-4-5 process of grading, luster is the second consideration for Mint State coins. *Luster* is the manner in which a coin reflects light.

Take a flashlight. Hold it up to a mirror and see how the mirror reflects the light. A proof coin—one with chromium-like surfaces—will often reflect the light the way the mirror did. Now envision the ocean. An ocean always reflects light, no matter what angle you look at it from, because of the many crevices and ridges on the surface of the water. No matter how you look at the ocean, it always reflects light. A Mint State coin reflects light in the same way, because that coin is manufactured with thousands of small striations which can't be seen with the naked eye. These tiny striations are called "flow lines," and they help give a Mint State coin its natural vibrant luster.

Go to the bank and get a shiny new penny. Chances are, it still has its original mint luster. That coin hasn't been spent, hasn't passed from hand to hand, and radiates the same original brilliance—the same appealing mint luster— it possessed the very day it was manufactured. But any coin, at any given time, is really in an intermediate stage between being completely brilliant and turning completely black. And this is especially true of Mint State coins.

Even if you took a coin on the day it was struck, carefully put it away, and meticulously preserved it, that coin would still progress from complete brilliance to total blackness. But the quality of that coin's mint brilliance, or luster—the manner in which it reflects light—would be an important determinant of its grade.

Some coins are said to be "toned," and this quality can be quite appealing. Keep in mind, however, that there's a very big difference between toning and tarnish.

Tarnish is the quick and irregular process by which a coin deteriorates over a short period of time. A copper coin stored in a moist environment could develop spots, for instance, in a matter of just a few days or even hours.

Toning is the slow and natural process by which a coin develops a patina over a period of months or years. If you took that same copper coin—the one that broke out in spots after being stored in a moist environment—and stored it instead in a dry environment, it could develop a beautiful protective patina over a period of many years.

Toning is actually an intermediate stage between complete brilliance—the way a coin looks right after being struck at the Mint—and complete blackness.

Many veteran collectors find toning extremely attractive. Novices, on the other hand, tend to think all coins should be bright and shiny—and, with that in mind, they often clean them. This is not just a bad idea; it's a *terrible* idea. It makes as much sense as lighting a match near spilled gasoline. Never, never, *never* clean your coins. If you were to take a brush and clean your coins, you would wear down the metal on their surfaces, and those coins would lose detail which could never be regained. This would be easily recognizable by numismatists, and would cause your coins' value to drop precipitously. What's more, the cleaning would activate the coins' surfaces chemically, causing them to deteriorate rapidly.

What *is* acceptable is a preservation process, but this should be left to experts. This process consists not of cleaning coins, but of neutralizing them for long-term storage. Consult your coin dealer for details.

Here are some guidelines regarding the impact of *luster* on grade:

- A coin can be designated Mint State-69 only if it has full and vibrant luster.
- A Mint State-67 coin has intense luster, emanating usually from surfaces that are immaculate.
- A Mint State-65 coin cannot be lackluster.
- A coin with the surfaces of an MS-67 coin but the mint

luster of an MS-65 might be deserving of the grade between those two: Mint State-66.
- A Mint State-63 coin may have toning that is not universally appealing.
- A Mint State-60 coin *can* be lackluster or dull.

In summary, if you have a coin that reflects mint luster
when you tilt and rotate it under a halogen lamp, and that
coin reflects light in the same way the ocean does, it is probably a true Mint State specimen. To determine its grade
more precisely, you should use the criteria outlined here.

TONING

As I have explained, toning is the color to which a coin turns
through sulfide reaction over the years. Certain types of
toning are universally attractive to numismatists and certain
other types are universally viewed as being ugly.

Concentric-circle toning can be exceedingly beautiful.
On a silver coin, for instance, you might see ocean blue
or rose red toning around the periphery fading into a
sunset-golden center. Such a coin would have universal
appeal because the toning is beautiful and original and
gives the coin a distinctive personality.

By contrast, a coin which is black—which looks as if
it has been exposed to the air for a long time—isn't nearly
as attractive. In fact, many numismatists might consider
it to be downright ugly.

Many new collectors think brilliance is best, but most
experienced hobbyists actually prefer coins with attractive
toning. Toning gives a coin its overall aesthetic appeal—its
eye appeal.

ARTIFICIAL TONING

Since toning is so desirable, certain unscrupulous people have devised ways of treating coins to give them the appearance of being naturally toned. The colors imparted to these coins by "artificial toning" may fool the uninitiated, but experienced individuals can spot it readily. Grading services will not certify coins with artificial toning.

To determine whether a coin has been artificially toned, study the coin's surfaces and underlying mint luster. In many instances, artificial toning is applied not only in an effort to simulate natural toning, but also to cover up an imperfection. On a Morgan silver dollar, for example, artificial toning may be used to divert attention from a large scrape on Miss Liberty's cheek. It also may be used to conceal the fact that a coin has been cleaned. This is another reason you should always examine a purportedly Mint State coin under a pinpoint light source such as a halogen lamp. If the coin has been cleaned, it won't reflect mint luster or reflect light properly when you tilt and rotate it under the lamp. That would be a good indication that the coin has been toned artificially.

Professional numismatists are adept at detecting artificial toning. Using their book knowledge, practical experience, and intuitive feel, they can often spot it a mile away. Obviously, that degree of skill can't be developed overnight. But, with a little practice, you too can become quite skillful. The key is to look beyond and beneath the toning. Look closely at the surfaces to see if you can find any imperfections, or see if there's a lack of mint luster. Follow these simple steps and before long you should be able to spot artificial toning with almost as much consistency as the pros.

STRIKE

Strike is the amount of detail a coin receives at the time
of its manufacture by the Mint. Some coins become worn
through being passed from hand to hand as people spend
them, but others exhibit a worn appearance from the very
moment they are made. Simply stated, all coins are not
created equal; some are manufactured without all the detail they're supposed to have. If a Mint State coin is not
fully struck, and therefore lacks details it was meant to
have, that coin will be assigned a lower grade.

Here are some points to remember with regard to *strike*:

- A Mint State-70 coin would have to be fully struck,
  since anything less than an absolutely full strike would
  render its appeal less than perfect. By extension, Mint
  State-68 and Mint State-69 coins also would require a
  full strike.
- A Mint State-65 coin cannot be weakly struck, although it can have a few areas which are not extremely
  sharply defined.
- A Mint State-64 coin *can* display some weakness of
  strike in key areas.
- A Mint State-63 coin doesn't necessarily have to be
  fully struck.

Logically, any coin grading higher than Mint State-65
would have to be well struck. On the other hand, any coin
grading lower than Mint State-63 would not have to exhibit a sharp strike.

EYE APPEAL

Eye appeal is the fifth and final element in our five-step grading process. This term refers to the overall appearance of a coin. Certain types of coins—coins with colorful, attractive toning, for example—are universally appealing to the eye. Others—coins with large nicks, gashes, or scratches or unattractive toning—are universally *unappealing*.

The concept of "eye appeal" applies not only to Mint State coins and proofs (see the following section), but also to circulated coins.

Circulated coins can have substantial eye appeal even if they're worn smooth from use, as long as the smoothness is uniform and the coins are free from defects. On the other hand, even a coin graded Very Fine—a relatively high level of preservation in the circulated range—can be very unattractive if it has a large gash which obliterates several letters in one of the mottos. That same coin would be desirable and eye-appealing if it were worn smoothly on both sides and had no visible problems.

Determining eye appeal can be quite subjective. Yet, there are certain constants. A Mint State coin with peripheral tonation rings is viewed by almost everyone as beautiful, for example, if the colors are attractive and the toning is natural. Few would dispute the eye appeal of a coin with an ocean-green periphery which fades into rings of sky blue, then into a very delicate rose-gold or sunset-tan center. Conversely, few would dispute the ugliness of a coin that looked as if a subway train had run over it, or a coin with black spots penetrating the surface.

Here's a basic rule of thumb: If a coin looks ugly to you, it probably is. In this case, beauty is very definitely in the eye of the beholder—and *you* are the beholder.

No matter how many coin dealers or certification services tell you that a coin merits a certain grade, follow your own intuition: If you don't like the way the coin looks, don't buy it. If, on the other hand, you think a certain coin is incredibly beautiful, chances are a lot of other people will agree with you. So always trust your instincts.

PROOF COINS

The term "proof" does not signify a grade or a level of preservation. Rather, it refers to the manner in which certain coins were manufactured. Proof coins are meant to be showpieces, so the Mint strikes them two or more times to give them greater detail than the coins it manufactures for circulation. Coins made for circulation are called "business-strike" coins.

Proof coins are sold by the Mint during their year of issue at a price that includes a premium over and above their face value. At this writing, the United States Mint is charging $12.50 for a current-year proof set of the five regularly issued U.S. coins (the cent, nickel, dime, quarter, and half dollar). Since the face value of these coins totals only 91 cents, the proof set's price includes an added premium of $11.59. (For information on ordering current proof sets directly from the Mint, write to: The United States Mint, P.O. Box 13576, Philadelphia, PA 19162-0011.)

Proof coins are graded on the same 1-to-70 scale as coins manufactured for circulation. Normally, proof coins do not enter circulation, and in such cases they are graded from 60 to 70, just like Mint State "business-strike" coins. However, some do circulate. Thus, it is possible for a proof coin—despite its shiny, chromium-like brilliance—

to have a grade below the Mint State range, between the numbers 1 and 59.

Proof coins are graded according to the number of "hairlines," or tiny pin scratches, visible on their surfaces. In order to grade a proof coin with any degree of accuracy, you will need a magnifying glass; a 5- or 7-power glass would be very helpful. A bright light would also assist you. Halogen lamps are especially useful in grading proof coins.

To grade a coin, proof or otherwise, you should hold the coin tightly between your thumb and forefinger and tilt and rotate that coin under a halogen lamp. Caution: When using a magnifying glass, be careful not to move the magnifying glass; move only the coin. When viewing a coin, you should tilt and rotate the coin, but always keep the magnifying glass in a stationary position under your eye.

A proof coin with many heavy hairlines is usually not very valuable. Such a coin often will be assigned a grade between 60 and 64. Proof coins relatively free from these tiny hairline scratches often will be graded 65 and above. Other differentials affecting proof coins will be discussed in the next section.

CIRCULATED COINS

In order to be considered truly Mint State, a coin must reflect light in a completely circular pattern when it is rotated under a pinpoint light source. Form a mental picture of a pencil-drawn circle and think of this as symbolizing a Mint State coin. If the circular pattern of reflection is not complete, the coin is not Mint State.

A not-quite Mint State coin will reflect light in an incomplete or disturbed pattern, as if a few small sections of the pencil-drawn circle had been erased. A cleaned coin will reflect light in a uniform pattern, all at once, with no trace of a circular pattern.

Coins which have very light friction on their highest points are said to be "About Uncirculated" (or "AU"). The numerical range from 50 to 59 has been set aside for grading these coins. At this time, however, only four of the ten numbers within that grading range are commonly used, and only these four are assigned by the grading services—and just three of the four are widely used. This reflects the fact that About Uncirculated coins trade within a relatively narrow price range compared with Mint State coins, so there isn't as great a need for pinpoint precision in grading them.

The numbers below 50 are set aside for coins in lesser grades—those below About Uncirculated. Throughout this range, no more than two numbers are commonly used for each grade because the marketplace doesn't require great precision.

When examining a circulated coin, you should make special note of its overall appeal. Ask yourself whether the coin is worn in an even manner, and check to see whether it has any nicks or scratches or other disturbing marks. Uniform wear enhances the appeal of a circulated coin, but unsightly imperfections detract from a coin's appearance and value.

Learning how to grade circulated coins may not be as vital from a profit-and-loss standpoint as mastering the grading of Mint State coins. Circulated coins tend to be priced much more modestly, and the variations in price from one grade to the next are far less drastic. Still, it's important to learn about these grades because almost all your pocket-change finds will be circulated coins, and knowing how to grade them will give you a better idea of their value.

There are two excellent books with valuable information on how to grade circulated coins. I highly recommend them as tools to help you hone your grading skills.

The first of these two books is *The Official ANA Grading Standards for United States Coins* by the American Numismatic Association (Western Publishing Company, Racine, WI 53404, 1987). This book provides step-by-step explanations of the grading guidelines for each major level of preservation and illustrates each grade with a line drawing. It encompasses every regular series of coins issued by the United States Mint since its inception.

The other book I recommend is *Photograde* by James F. Ruddy (Bowers and Merena Galleries, Wolfeboro, NH 03894, 1989). This covers much of the same ground as the ANA grading guide, but does so with photographs, rather than drawings. *Photograde* deals only with circulated coins, in grades from About Good to About Uncirculated. The ANA guide, by contrast, deals with Mint State coins, as well.

Grade-sensitive areas are the portions of coins where even small imperfections can have a significant impact on the grading of those coins. It's important to be familiar with these areas. If a coin has a small scratch on its back, no one may really notice it very much—but if the same size scratch were on the *front* of the coin, right on the face of Miss Liberty, for example, that coin might be assigned a lower grade than the coin with the scratch on the back.

Coin grading is a subjective process, but there *are* certain parameters which the grading services have set forth, and these permit general agreement on grade.

Following are the major circulated grades:

About Uncirculated (AU-50)

Obverse: Only a trace of wear will show on the highest points such as above the ear and the lowest curl of hair.

Reverse: Only a trace of wear will show on the highest points of the leaves and ribbon bow.

Lincoln Head Cents
1909 to date

About Good (AG-3)

Obverse: The rim will be worn down into the letters. Date and mint-mark will be weak but readable.

Reverse (1909-1958): The rim will be worn down into the letters and the wheat stalks.

Good (G-4)

Obverse: Letters in the legend may be touching the rim. The date will be full.

Reverse (1909-1958): The wheat stalks will be worn smooth but distinctly outlined.

Very Good (VG-8)

Obverse: All letters in the legend will be sharp and clear. A few hair details will begin to show.

Reverse (1909-1958): About half of the lines in the upper wheat stalks will show.

Fine (F-12)

Obverse: Lincoln's ear and bow tie will be clearly visible.

Reverse (1909-1958): The parallel lines in the upper wheat stalks will show plainly and be separated even though worn. One side or the other may show a weak area at the top of the stalk.

Good (G-4)

Obverse: The outline of the Indian will be distinct. "LIBERTY" will not show on the headband. The rim may be worn down to the tops of the letters.

Reverse: The wreath will be completely outlined but worn flat.

Very Good (VG-8)

Obverse: A total of any three letters of "LIBERTY" will show. This can be a combination of two full letters plus two half letters as not all dates of Indian cents wore uniformly.

Reverse: The wreath will begin to show some detail. *Note: The bottom of the "N" in "ONE" may be weak due to striking.*

Fine (F-12)

Obverse: A full "LIBERTY" will be visible but it will not be sharp.

Reverse: The top part of the leaves will be worn smooth. The ribbon bow will show considerable wear.

Very Fine (VF-20)

Obverse: A full sharp "LIBERTY" will be visible even though there is some wear. The feathers will be worn on the tips. *Note: Indian cents cannot be graded by the diamond designs on the ribbon as this feature was not always sharply struck.*

Reverse: There will be more detail in the leaves and ribbon bow.

Extremely Fine (EF-40)

Obverse: There must be a full sharp "LIBERTY." The ends of the feathers (except on certain weakly struck issues, such as 1859-1864 copper-nickel pieces) will be sharply detailed.

Reverse: There will be wear on the high points of the leaves and ribbon bow.

2 pages from the popular trade book, Photograde, *by James F. Ruddy (Copyright 1988 by Bowers & Merena Galleries, Inc.). Simply match your coin to the photograph and—presto—it's graded.*

- About Uncirculated-58 (AU-58).

  An AU-58 coin appears at first glance to be Mint State and betrays only very small signs of wear when examined more closely. You will see just the slightest evidence of wear or friction on the very highest points of the coin. Take a Lincoln cent out of your pocket and look at Abe Lincoln's face; look at his cheek and jaw. These are the highest points on the Lincoln cent. Envision a brand-new coin that you just got from the bank being spent by one or two people, and picture that coin sliding around briefly in their pockets. That's the kind of coin that probably would be graded AU-58.

- About Uncirculated-55 (AU-55).

  Almost all the mint luster remains on an AU-55 coin, but signs of circulation are slightly more visible than on its AU-58 counterpart.

- About Uncirculated-50 (AU-50).

  On an AU-50 coin, signs of slight wear are visible not only on the highest points, but throughout. On that Lincoln cent you took from your pocket, for example, you would notice a great deal more detail missing from the cheek and the jaw than if the coin were AU-55. On an AU-50 coin, considerable wear is also visible in the areas which are *not* raised above the surface— the right and left "fields," where there isn't any writing. However, much mint luster still adheres, so you will see patches of the original color—the color you normally see on a coin that you've just gotten fresh from the bank, one that hasn't circulated. These patches usually adhere around the area which is raised on the coin.

- Extremely Fine-45 (EF-45).

  Light wear is visible throughout the highest points of

a coin graded EF-45. But, while the coin displays significant wear, very small signs of mint luster can still be seen. Basically, this is a coin which has passed through many hands yet hasn't lost too much of its detail.

- Extremely Fine-40 (EF-40).

    EF-40 is the less desirable Extremely Fine grade. An EF-40 coin is worn a little more than its EF-45 counterpart, or has some type of nick or scratch which makes it less desirable.

- Very Fine-30 (VF-30).

    On a coin grading VF-30, considerable wear will be visible throughout. Areas which are supposed to display certain details will appear worn down. However, these details will not be completely lost. Abe Lincoln's hair on the cent, for example, will still display some of the original details that the Mint intended the coin to have when it was new. Details will look worn on many portions of the coin, but will still be somewhat visible.

- Very Fine-20 (VF-20).

    A VF-20 coin is not as desirable as its VF-30 counterpart, possibly because it has some detracting characteristic. It might have a nick or scratch, for example—so that while it is the equal of the VF-30 coin in every other respect, the imperfection knocks down its grade to VF-20. Or it might be just a little more worn than the VF-30 coin, but not worn enough to be downgraded to Fine.

- Fine-12.

    On a Fine-12 coin, the basic design is visible and identifiable, but there's very substantial wear throughout. Many coins which are circulated—the kinds of coins you are likely to find in your piggy bank—would be graded Fine-12. Likewise, this is the grade that pertains to many of the silver coins that turn up in old accumulations.

Since Fine-12 is such a common grade, let's consider a few examples drawn from *The Official ANA Grading Standards for United States Coins*.

The ANA guide tells us that a Fine-12 Mercury dime (a coin produced from 1916 to 1945) has "moderate to considerable even wear," and that the entire design is "clear and bold." On the obverse (or "heads" side), it says, "some details" show in Liberty's hair; all the feathers "are weak but partially visible"; and the hair braid "is nearly worn away." On the reverse, the ANA guide states, the vertical lines in the fasces—the bundle of rods depicted on the coin—"are all visible but lack sharpness" and, while the diagonal bands show on the fasces, one is worn smooth at the midpoint.

Describing a Fine-12 Standing Liberty quarter (a coin produced from 1916 to 1930), the ANA guide states that on the obverse, the details of Miss Liberty's gown are worn, but "show clearly" across her body. The left leg is lightly worn, the book tells us, while the right leg is nearly flat and the toe is worn. On the coin's reverse, we are told, the breast of the eagle is "worn almost smooth" but half of the wing feathers "are visible, although well worn in spots."

In writing about the Lincoln cent, the ANA grading guide says Fine-12 examples have "moderate to heavy even wear" and the entire design "is clear and bold." On the obverse, it says, "some details show in the hair," while the cheek and jaw "are worn nearly smooth." The inscription *LIBERTY* shows clearly, we are told, with no letters missing, and Lincoln's ear and bow are both visible. On the reverse, the grading guide says, most details are visible in the wheat stalks and the top wheat lines "are worn but separated."

- Very Good-8 (VG-8).

  A VG-8 coin is identifiable as to its type, but extremely well worn. The design lacks many of the details that the Mint intended the coin to have. The features which stand out from the surface of the coin are visible, but many of the details have been worn flat.

- Good-4 (Good).

  In describing coins they have, people often say they're in "good condition." Actually, "Good" condition is one of the very *lowest* levels of preservation. Coins in Good condition have an extraordinary degree of wear. They've passed through thousands—possibly even millions—of hands. Coins in Good condition have considerable wear on every part, and very little detail is left. The rim is still basically intact.

- About Good-3 (AG-3).

  On an AG-3 coin, most of the rim is worn away and much of the design has also been lost because the coin has passed through so many hands.

Although the grading system employs a numerical scale from 1 to 70, numbers lower than 3 are seldom used. Coins with grades that low are essentially worthless as collectibles, except in the case of great rarities.

CHAPTER 7

TRADING COINS LIKE STOCKS

Buying and selling many rare coins today is sometimes like buying and selling shares of common stock.

When you buy five shares of a popular stock such as Xerox or Federal Express, those shares are said to be "fungible." That means they duplicate each other—they're alike and they're traded in like-kind units. You can buy five shares of Federal Express and sell five shares of Federal Express and on each end you'll have a relatively clean paper transaction, facilitated by computer technology and the magnetic media to which we're so accustomed in this modern electronic age.

Rare coins can now be traded in very similar fashion. Let's suppose, for instance, that you buy five 1881-S Morgan dollars (silver dollars made in 1881 at the San Francisco Mint, with an "S" below the eagle on the reverse). And let's say these coins are graded Mint State-65 and cost you $100 apiece. Six months later, if 1881-S Morgan dollars graded Mint State-65 have increased in value to $150 apiece, you'll be able to sell any or all of your five coins for $150 each just as if they were shares of your favorite stock.

Rare coins didn't always enjoy this high degree of liquidity. What gives it to them today is a process known as "coin certification." In recent years, we have witnessed the development of highly skilled "certification services"—companies which, for a fee, will render an opinion as to a coin's grade, or level of preservation, on the 1-through-70 scale.

After assigning a grade to a coin, these services encapsulate that coin in a tamper-resistant, sonically sealed, hard plastic holder, along with a small paper insert which indicates the level of preservation. Coins encased in such holders are said to have been "certified." The grade assigned to a coin by a certification service gives buyers and sellers a reasonable ballpark idea as to its level of preservation, and some dealers might even make a sight-unseen offer for such a coin, based upon its certified grade.

Remember what I said earlier:

As of this writing, the three leading certification services—the ones which can be relied upon most for the consistency and accuracy of their grading standards—are the Numismatic Guaranty Corporation of America (NGC), based in Parsippany, New Jersey, the Professional Coin Grading Service (PCGS) in Newport Beach, California, and ANACS of Columbus, Ohio.

The founder of PCGS, coin dealer David Hall, is the man who devised the system of encapsulating coins and trading them sight-unseen. This system is now accepted and used throughout the rare coin industry. NGC soon followed suit under the direction of John Albanese, a professional numismatist widely respected for his knowledge and integrity.

Right from the inception of NGC, Albanese has taken a strong consumer protection stance. To reassure consumers that no conflict of interest exists in NGC's grading practices, he initially prohibited the company's principals from buying or selling coins.

PCGS is owned by coin dealers and they remain active in the market. However, PCGS's published anti–self-interest policy prohibits anyone who actively trades coins from grading for it. In fact, the company has achieved tremendous acceptance, and its grading judgments are highly respected.

ANACS came into being as an arm of the American Numismatic Association, the world's largest coin club. In 1990, the ANA sold its grading service to Amos Press of Sidney, Ohio, publisher of *Coin World* and other hobby periodicals.

Grading coins is subjective, but PCGS, NGC, and ANACS bring relative consistency to the process—and a high degree of accuracy—by using a consensus approach. Coins submitted for evaluation are examined by several different graders, and if the majority agree upon a grade, that's the one assigned.

All three services accept coins from the public for certification. However, coins can be submitted to NGC only through authorized submission centers. PCGS accepts coins directly from any ANA member; others must submit them through a PCGS submission center. ANACS accepts direct submissions from anyone. To obtain information about the services, including a free list of submission centers, write to them as follows:

Numismatic Guaranty Corporation of America Inc.
P.O. Box 1776
Parsippany, NJ 07054

Professional Coin Grading Service
P.O. Box 9458
Newport Beach, CA 92658

ANACS
P.O. Box 182141
Columbus, OH 43218-2141

COMPUTER GRADING

Although consensus grading by expert human graders
has been extremely successful, the major certification
services have spent considerable time, effort, and money
exploring the possible use of computers to make their
results even more consistent and accurate. In May 1990,
PCGS began using a computer—dubbed *The Expert*—to
help grade Morgan silver dollars.

The Expert simulated human thought processes and,
from early indications, was able to grade coins consistently in accordance with the standards established for
Morgan dollars by PCGS.

This noble experiment has suspended, but it provided
considerable food for thought.

The Expert graded coins on a step-by-step basis,
very much the way human graders do. Indeed, it was
programmed with information gleaned from the experts on the PCGS staff. Much can be learned from
reviewing these steps, for knowing what's involved
in determining a grade can help us become better
graders ourselves—and smarter buyers. You should
familiarize yourself with the computer's "thought
process" so that you can use the same approach yourself.

According to information provided by PCGS, *The
Expert* graded each coin on the basis of the following
steps:

1. **Image capture.**

   Multiple images of the coin, obtained under various lighting conditions, are captured in digital form, using a special camera. Looking at this in human terms, it's equivalent to tilting and rotating the coin under a halogen lamp to search for imperfections.

2. **Image enhancement.**

   All of the captured images—or the most significant ones—are computer-enhanced to bring out important features of the coin. In human terms, this is the equivalent of using a magnifying glass to examine the coin carefully.

3. **Low-frequency marks analysis.**

   The key areas of the coin are examined in great detail to identify, classify, measure, and score all flaws. This is similar to using the magnifying glass to scrutinize the most important areas of the coin for scratches and other imperfections.

4. **High-frequency marks analysis.**

   Secondary portions of the coin are examined to identify flaws that exist in busy background areas such as the hair, letters, and rim. These flaws are then classified, measured, and scored by the computer, and it takes them into consideration when assigning a grade. This is what you do yourself when you check the areas which aren't of prime importance on the coin when you're grading it or looking for imperfections.

5. **Mirror and luster.**

   A light-flow and reflectance analysis is used to precisely measure the "mirror," or reflective quality, of the coin, as well as its inherent luster. This is of particular importance on special silver dollars which are said to be *prooflike*.

Prooflike silver dollars (and their counterparts in other coin series) look like proof coins—coins produced by a special slow process with multiple strikings and brilliant, mirrorlike surfaces. In reality, however, they're unusually bright and attractive "business-strike" coins, the kind intended for use in circulation.

Prooflike Morgan dollars enjoy an especially wide following among collectors. These coins have reflective backgrounds (fields) and frosted raised parts (devices). Frequently, the contrast between the fields (the background areas of a coin) and the raised parts—such as the portrait, the stars, the date, and the lettering—creates a lovely cameo look.

To the untrained eye, a prooflike coin looks very much like a proof, just as its name suggests. Its brilliant, mirrorlike surface lends particular credence to this notion. But the PCGS computer is capable of distinguishing a prooflike Morgan dollar from a proof.

6. **Strike.**

Key areas of the coin are examined to measure the strength of the strike. One of these areas is Miss Liberty's hair, especially the portion above her ear.

7. **Eye appeal.**

Dozens of aspects of the coin are examined to define such qualities as satin smoothness, light flow, "flash," color, and toning—aspects that serve to establish the mood or eye appeal of the coin. (See the previous chapter for a detailed discussion of eye appeal.)

8. **Synthesis.**

The computer draws upon thousands of parameters—constant values for various grades—which have been stored in its memory, and synthesizes these with the key components of the coin. Among the factors evaluated during this process are front and back nicks or other flaws, strike, luster, eye appeal, mirror surface, toning, key-area metrics, and exceptional conditions.

9. **Final grade.**

The results of synthesis are then combined, using a complex set of master rules to establish the final grade for the coin.

COIN GRADING SCAMS

Leading coin grading services have broadened rare coins' acceptance and credibility throughout the investment community with their strict, consistent grading and their incorruptible judgments. However, there have been many copycats, and some of these are far less reliable, far less consistent, and not nearly as honest.

Some of the other coin-grading organizations *are* honest and consistent but, by their own admission, they grade according to standards which aren't nearly as strict as those set forth by PCGS, NGC, and ANACS. One such service which deserves particular mention is the Numismatic Certification Institute (NCI).

NCI is owned by a very large coin company, the Heritage Capital Corporation of Dallas, Texas. Heritage admits that NCI's grading standards are about one point more liberal than those of NGC and PCGS. But this doesn't mean that NCI is bad. In fact, there are many people who collect NCI-graded coins exclusively. NCI is a highly respected service and is not to be confused with scam operators. But you should beware of con men who try to sell you NCI coins and use a pricing structure intended for coins from PCGS and NGC. Because the grading of NCI coins is more liberal, their prices are lower than those of comparably graded coins from the two leading services.

The following chart will give you an idea of the comparable values of coins that have been graded by various certification services. In each case, the price shown is the fair market value, as of October 1995, for an 1881-S Morgan dollar graded Mint State-65. Keep in mind that while the *grade* is the same in each case, the actual condition—or level of preservation—of the coin you would receive may vary considerably from one service to another, since some use much stricter standards. The stricter and more consistent the standards, the higher the price will normally be.

This list should provide you with guidance as to which services have strict grading standards and which have standards that simply don't make the grade.

Grading Service	October 1995 Fair Market Retail Value for 1881-S Morgan Dollar in MS-65
Numismatic Guaranty Corporation of America	$80
Professional Coin Grading Service	80
ANACS/Amos Press, Inc.	78
Numismatic Certification Institute	50
International Numismatic Society Authentication Bureau, Washington, DC	40
Grading Service "X" (many—beware!)	20

RESUMBISSIONS

Dealers sometimes remove certified coins from their plastic holders and resubmit the coins to the same grading service or a different service in hopes that they will receive higher grades. In the great majority of cases, these resubmitted coins come back the second time with the same grade. Occasionally, though, "borderline" coins—those at the high end of one grade—will be upgraded to the next higher level.

There is strong incentive to resubmit certain coins, since the difference in value between one grade and the next—between Mint State-64 and Mint State-65, for example—can be many hundreds of dollars. There is nothing unethical about this practice, but buyers and sellers should be aware of it. In time, as computer grading is perfected, we will see far fewer resubmissions and they will be far less successful.

TRADING COINS LIKE STOCKS

All certified coins can be—and are—traded in much the same way as stocks. In practice, however, those most commonly traded sight-unseen are the coins which are most fungible—those which exist in relatively large quantities in Mint State-65 and Mint State-64 condition, the two grades most favored by the broad spectrum of investors. These include common-date Morgan silver dollars, Saint-Gaudens double eagles, and Walking Liberty half dollars.

Extremely rare coins—those costing, say, $25,000 or more—can certainly be traded sight-unseen, and on many occasions they are. However, these coins are more likely to be scrutinized, and bought on a "sight-seen" basis, by a prospective purchaser.

The coins most likely to be traded like shares of stock are popular issues with many "like-kind units"—coins which exist in relatively large numbers in high, investment-quality grades.

Independent certification of rare coins, while recommended, does not guarantee protection against the normal risks associated with volatile markets. The degree of liquidity for certified coins will vary according to general market conditions and the particular coin involved. For some coins, there may be *no active market at all* at certain points in time.

WALL STREET'S FLIRTATION WITH THE COIN MARKET

The rare coin market built up tremendous momentum during the 1980s. Annual surveys by Salomon Brothers, a respected New York City brokerage firm, consistently found rare coins to be among the most rewarding investment vehicles, regularly outperforming more conventional forms such as stocks and bonds. Thousands of investors with little or no knowledge about coins began to include them in their portfolios—and this, in turn, led seasoned Wall Street professionals to take a closer look at the phenomenon. Apparently, they liked what they saw, for as the decade neared a close, several major brokerages were actively involved with coin-related investment funds or poised to take the plunge.

A *Business Week* article reported at the time that investors were "flipping over the coin market." And it wasn't hard to understand why. Over a short period in 1989, rare coins were acknowledged to have increased in value a remarkable 40 percent. The rocket ride was propelled, to a great extent, by coin certification and sight-unseen trading.

A number of high-powered brokers came to view certified coins as being much like stocks in their liquidity. Once a major grading service vouched for the grade of a coin and sealed that coin in an airtight plastic holder, would-be buyers all around the country stood ready and willing to buy it—without even having seen and examined it first—at a price level established by the marketplace.

Merrill Lynch was the first big Wall Street firm to put its prestige and resources behind a coin investment fund. In 1986, it established the Athena Fund, a limited-partnership fund which used investors' shares to purchase $7 million worth of ancient coins and antiquities. Encouraged by the initial success of this venture, it launched a second one—Athena Fund II—in 1988, this time with $25 million. In both instances, investors bought shares, and managers appointed by Merrill Lynch used the pooled resources to acquire rare coins and antiquities. The idea was to sell these in five to seven years and divvy up the profits among the investor partners.

In 1989, Kidder, Peabody announced plans for a $40 million limited-partnership fund featuring U.S. coins, and that drove already-rising coin prices to even greater heights. Then, as now, U.S. coins occupied center stage in the rare-coin marketplace, and the prospect of having tens of millions of dollars spent in this pivotal area triggered a buying spree even more dramatic than Merrill Lynch's ancient coin purchases had done. Traders rushed to accumulate desirable coins, anticipating massive new activity and price gains.

Unfortunately for them, May 1989 turned out to be not the starting point of a big new surge, but rather the very zenith of an upward market cycle that was running out of steam. Almost at once, prices began to soften and slip, and analysts quickly recognized that the boom of the 1980s had gone too far, too fast. Wall Street's flirtation with coins had created unrealistic expectations and driven prices unreasonably high for many coins that weren't especially rare. Common-date silver dollars in very high levels of preservation—while certainly aesthetically appealing—often were available by the thousands, for example, so it didn't make sense for them to carry huge premiums.

While some firms and individuals in the traditional financial community had dallied with rare coins during the late 1980s, others had viewed this relationship with suspicion. These skeptics felt relief—and a sense of vindication—when coin prices started to falter. The skid accelerated when the overall U.S. economy entered a deep recession in the early 1990s. And the downturn worsened when firms such as Merrill Lynch and Kidder, Peabody turned their backs on rare coins, breaking off their courtship when the going began to get rough. This dealt a severe psychological blow to the coin market, and had the ironic side effect of sharply reducing the value of the coins in those companies' limited-partnership funds.

Wall Street brought undeniable excitement to the coin market, along with the potential for spectacular price gains. The excitement lasted only briefly, and the price potential was never fully realized. But they have given way to stability and a greater sense of proportion. Today's expectations may be more modest, but they're also more realistic. The coin market may not have stars in its eyes anymore, but it has its feet on the ground—and with or without Wall Street, there's ample cause to be bullish about its future.

MARKET CYCLES

Fungible, generic coins such as common-date Morgan silver dollars and Saint-Gaudens double eagles ($20 gold pieces) tend to follow definite market cycles. They move up and down in value within fairly regular ranges of price and time.

By tracking these cycles and timing your buy-and-sell activity to coincide with the market's valleys and peaks, you can reap some handsome profits. You might, for example, purchase an 1881-S silver dollar graded Mint State-65 for $85 at the market low, then sell it within a matter of months for twice that amount when the cycle turns upward.

The following chart will give you a good idea of how coins can rise in value dramatically during a short period. The prices listed here show how twenty-seven of the most popularly traded Morgan dollars rose in value between March 24, 1989, and May 19, 1989. The valuations have been taken from the *Certified Coin Dealer Newsletter*, which used the American Numismatic Exchange as its source. These coins declined in value dramatically after their meteoric rise.

COIN (DATE AND MINT-MARK)	GRADE	POPULATION: PCGS/NGC	3/24/89 VALUE	5/19/89 VALUE	CHANGE
Morgan Dollars					
1878-S	MS-64	2,991/558	$ 125	$160	+28%
	MS-65	858/222	685	830	+21%
1879-S	MS-64	10,678/2,305	97	160	+65%
	MS-65	7,109/1,496	310	535	+73%
1880-CC	MS-64	1,012/138	307	405	+32%
	MS-65	336/34	1,850	2,350	+27%

1880-S	MS-64	15,584/3,013	97	155	+60%
	MS-65	10,730/1,958	310	535	+73%
1881-CC	MS-64	1,861/241	360	400	+11%
	MS-65	903/93	970	1,240	+28%
1881-S	MS-64	28,046/4,757	100	155	+55%
	MS-65	17,236/2,989	310	535	+73%
1882	MS-64	1,116/276	220	245	+11%
	MS-65	235/39	1,385	1,775	+28%
1882-CC	MS-64	2,658/227	185	225	+22%
	MS-65	920/88	845	1,000	+18%
1882-S	MS-64	9,132/1,806	99	160	+62%
	MS-65	5,519/1,245	310	535	+73%
1883	MS-64	2,740/349	102	160	+57%
	MS-65	1,297/149	530	820	+55%
1883-CC	MS-64	3,925/422	180	215	+19%
	MS-65	1,656/173	675	900	+33%
1883-O	MS-64	6,871/1,055	105	155	+48%
	MS-65	1,666/304	405	680	+68%
1884	MS-64	1,532/243	120	160	+33%
	MS-65	543/72	710	1,110	+56%
1884-CC	MS-64	3,963/388	175	230	+31%
	MS-65	1,423/121	690	900	+30%
1884-O	MS-64	11,178/1,675	98	155	+58%
	MS-65	2,895/411	315	535	+70%
1885	MS-64	5,212/846	99	160	+62%
	MS-65	2,165/438	322	555	+72%
1885-CC	MS-64	1,649/227	390	410	+ 5%
	MS-65	720/80	1,340	1,760	+31%
1885-O	MS-64	13,354/2,078	99	155	+57%
	MS-65	4,504/943	315	535	+70%
1886	MS-64	9,422/1,557	100	160	+60%
	MS-65	4,125/747	315	535	+70%
1887	MS-64	11,745/2,082	100	160	+60%
	MS-65	3,756/901	310	535	+73%
1888	MS-64	3,000/513	120	160	+33%
	MS-65	804/179	665	895	+35%
1888-O	MS-64	1,265/236	180	235	+30%
	MS-65	257/45	1,720	2,025	+18%

COIN (DATE AND MINT-MARK)	GRADE	POPULATION: PCGS/NGC	3/24/89 VALUE	5/19/89 VALUE	CHANGE
Morgan Dollars					
1889	MS-64	1,633/494	155	210	+35%
	MS-65	233/50	1,800	1,900	+ 5%
1890-S	MS-64	576/113	325	365	+12%
	MS-65	145/25	1,510	2,000	+32%
1896	MS-64	2,828/599	104	160	+54%
	MS-65	774/176	685	995	+45%
1897	MS-64	1,361/241	150	160	+ 7%
	MS-65	315/41	1,140	1,500	+32%
1897-S	MS-64	736/204	225	285	+27%
	MS-65	230/74	980	1,350	+38%

THE SCOTT TRAVERS EIGHT-STEP MARKET-CYCLE BUY-SELL PLAN, OR HOW TO MAKE A FORTUNE IN COINS IN EIGHT EASY STEPS

Earlier, I showed you how to use three simple steps to gauge the current psychology, or "temperature," of the coin market. Following is a list of eight easy guidelines to help you take advantage of this knowledge—and predictable market cycles—to maximize your profits from rare coins.

1. Follow market cycles.

Determine the low and high points for any particular coin in which you may be interested. In an active market, many coins trade within definite ranges. For example, in the late 1980s, that a number of common-date Morgan silver dollars graded Mint State-65 tend to move up and down within a trading range from $100 to $500.

You can get a good feel for how the market performs by studying past issues of the *Coin Dealer Newsletter*, a weekly publication—widely referred to as the "Greysheet"—that lists the current values of all commonly traded U.S. coins. Examine a number of Greysheets covering a period of several months and you'll start to see a pricing pattern emerge. You can obtain a book with many past issues for $24.95 postpaid by writing to the *Coin Dealer Newsletter*, P.O. Box 11099, Torrance, CA 90510.

2. **Locate and identify large coin promoters.**

A number of very large coin companies run regular promotions featuring certain types of coins. Two such companies are Blanchard & Co. Inc. of Louisiana, and Investment Rarities Inc. of Minneapolis.

Whenever these companies promote a particular coin or series of coins, the surge of activity will cause their prices to rise in the market at large. Let's say, for example, that Blanchard is promoting Liberty Head eagles ($10 gold pieces) graded Mint State-65. In conducting its promotion, the company will distribute advertisements to many thousands of prospective purchasers urging them to buy these coins. That, in turn, will generate demand which will put upward pressure on the prices of *all* Mint State-65 Liberty Head eagles.

Your key to making a profit is to *sell* the kinds of coins that are being promoted. Keep in mind that the market for these coins is probably at its peak during the time the promotions are being run. Once the advertisements stop, demand will decrease and prices will fall.

What you must do is *anticipate* which coins will be coming up for promotion and buy some before the campaign begins. To do so, you should get on the mailing lists of large coin companies that run these types of promotions. Then, pick out a popular coin that these dealers are likely to promote but which they are *not* promoting at the moment. Check to see whether that coin is at the low or high end of its market cycle, following the approach outlined in Step 1. If it's at the low end, the time is probably right to buy some, since this coin has two big pluses: Its market cycle is due to head back up and it's due to be promoted.

3. **Actually buy the coin.**

When the time comes to actually make a purchase, ask your dealer to check the current buy and sell prices on the Certified Coin Exchange (CCE). This is a sophisticated electronic trading mechanism which enables buyers and sellers worldwide—dealers, collectors, and investors alike—to determine what the ballpark value of any particular certified coin is at a given time. Dealers trade coins among themselves on this system. Be careful. If a dealer on CCE is offering a certain coin for sale at $1,000, but the three highest offers to buy that kind of coin are only $100, you need to find out why. Are the buy offers too low, or is the sale price too high?

Another excellent way to keep track of sight-unseen prices for certified coins is to purchase the *Certified Coin Dealer Newsletter*. This weekly publication, popularly known as the "Bluesheet," is available by subscription at a rate of six months for

$65. The address is P.O. Box 11099, Torrance, CA 90510.

Coins in the very highest grades have performed the best, and coins grading 65 are the most popular. Keep in mind, however, that while popularly traded generic coins—common-date Morgan silver dollars graded Mint State-65, for example—can make you a lot of money, some of the rarer coins might make you a lot *more* money.

4. **Don't get scared.**

The coin market can be extraordinarily volatile. This will make it harder to anticipate the direction of the market, and heighten the odds that you'll guess wrong now and then, even though you've done all your homework perfectly. You may find that instead of going *up* in price, a coin you have identified as a good bet for promotion or cyclical gain actually goes *down*.

This doesn't mean you should immediately sell that coin and lose money. Often, such coins will bounce right back in a matter of just a few days. In fact, this may be a prime opportunity to acquire more specimens.

Psychologically, the low point of the market is one of the most difficult times for people to buy. But, in fact, that's when the market is really the strongest—and the high point is when it's the weakest. Only after a market cycle has run its course do most people look back and see what was really happening. Often, the time when people have the greatest resistance to buying is when market values are at the bottom and things look bleak—yet that's when they should really be buying the most.

5. Continue to accumulate.

The Professional Coin Grading Service, the Numismatic Guaranty Corporation, and ANACS all issue periodic reports listing the number of coins of each type, date, and mint mark that they have certified in the various grade levels. Check these reports to see which coins have low "populations" (as PCGS calls them) or "censuses" (the equivalent term used by NGC). This will help guide you in determining which coins you should buy, for coins of which fewer examples have been certified are likely to appreciate in value more rapidly.

Your accumulation period should be a time of extreme caution, and you should limit your purchases to coins which have been independently certified by PCGS, NGC, or ANACS.

6. Take your profit.

By the time you reach this point, some of the coins you accumulated in Step 5 may have risen in value appreciably. For that matter, some of the coins you bought in Step 3 (and possibly saw decline in value in Step 4) may also be showing handsome gains. Perhaps certain coins you purchased for $250 each are now selling for $500. Now is the time to cash in some of these chips.

Use your intuition. But, if you see a tidy profit, don't hesitate. Sell. *If you see that you've achieved an impressive profit, go to the cash window and celebrate.*

If something rises in value dramatically in a very short period, that increase may be the result of an artificial run-up or some other temporary phenomenon. When you see an immediate run-up, that—more than ever—is the time to consider selling right away.

The coin market operates in a series of condensed, contracted boom-and-bust cycles which take anywhere from two months to two years to run their course. At times, a coin will go up from $150 to $500, then down to $150 again, within a matter of just a few months. Other times, it may take a couple of years for this process to be completed.

7. **Cash out nonperformers.**

If you're not prepared to hold out for the long term, don't let your ego blind you to reality. Take your loss and go on to something else that will be a better performer in the current marketplace.

A coin can be considered a nonperformer if it hasn't increased in value over an extended period and in fact has a long-term trend of *decreasing* in value.

8. **Use your common sense.**

Whether you're buying or selling, trust your judgment. Don't let a dealer sway you by building up a coin or knocking it down. If the coin looks ugly to you, don't buy it. And if a coin you're selling looks extremely attractive to you, don't let the dealer convince you it has problems, and don't accept less than you think it's worth. The dealer may be trying to take advantage of you. Shop around and look for a higher offer; don't be afraid to go to a second dealer and ask what *he* would pay. Use your common sense—and your own sensibility.

There you have it: the Scott Travers eight-step buy–sell plan. Continue to perform these eight simple steps and you have an excellent chance to make a lot of money over an extended period.

Obviously, you'll need more expertise to take full advantage of marketplace situations and opportunities. For a more detailed discussion of how to buy and sell coins, I urge you to read one of my earlier books, *The Investor's Guide to Coin Trading* (John Wiley & Sons Inc., 1990). This will take you behind the scenes in the rare coin market and equip you with the knowledge you need to be successful in complex marketplace situations.

Coin Universe Home Page on the World Wide Web. *Set your Internet browser to: http://www.coin-universe.com for the coolest starting point in numismatics. (Photo courtesy InfoExchange, Inc.)*

COINS, COMPUTERS, AND THE INTERNET

The Computer Revolution is rapidly transforming virtually every aspect of American life, and coin collecting is very much caught up in the excitement and the change. Indeed, the applications of computer technology seem certain to have an increasingly profound impact on the hobby—and the business of buying and selling coins—as we enter the new millennium.

The marriage of coins and computers first manifested itself during the 1980s with the establishment of computerized coin trading networks which facilitated the trading of coins on a sight-unseen basis. Sight-unseen trading diminished significantly during the first part of the 1990s, when lingering malaise in the rare-coin marketplace led to the departure of many big-money investors, who had been the principal buyers of such material. And this, in turn, greatly reduced the need for computer trading networks.

By the mid-1990s, however, the Computer Revolution was influencing rare coins, and the people who collect them, in even more personal and fundamental ways. By then, many millions of Americans had linked up with each other through on-line computer services, and this was giving coin collectors—and hobby organizations—a powerful new method to communicate among themselves and reach out to potential new recruits. It also loomed large as a marketing tool for dealers and a vehicle to expedite trading among collectors.

All you need is a computer and a modem to access an on-line service, where an answering modem connects you to that service. You can communicate online with users from all around the nation and even the world. (Generally, the call is local, so no long-distance telephone charges are incurred.) Once on-line, you can access vast stores of information compiled for the membership of the on-line service. Alternatively, you can communicate with others by sending and receiving electronic messages, or "e-mail."

The ultimate "information superhighway" is the Internet, a loosely connected universe of computer networks and bulletin boards that brings together data on just about every conceivable aspect of human experience. The Internet encompasses more than 6,000 separate "newsgroups," or series of public messages and responses about related topics. The hottest place in cyberspace, however, is the Internet's World Wide Web, where a click of the mouse on hyperlinked text lets you visit any area of interest.

Originally developed as a means of communication between the U.S. military establishment and scientific researchers at institutions of higher learning, the Internet now serves a fast-growing segment of the general public. According to some estimates, nearly thirty million persons from the United States and Canada are surfing the Internet. Software and dial-up connections are available from various Internet service providers, and the only cost beyond the initial outlay is usually a flat monthly fee—typically about $20. By contrast, on-line services such as America Online, CompuServe, Prodigy, and Genie—while offering access to the Internet—charge according to usage, and this can add up to hundreds of dollars a month, even at a modest-sounding rate of $2.95 per hour.

THE MEDIUM AND THE MESSAGE

Growing numbers of coin organizations and individuals are utilizing the Internet and/or on-line services to publicize themselves and their activities. They do this by establishing "web sites" or "bulletin boards" where Internet surfers and on-line members can access information they provide. The American Numismatic Association (ANA), the nation's largest coin club, has been in the forefront of this fast-growing movement. In June 1993, the ANA went on-line with CompuServe and Prodigy, giving it a forum in a vibrant new marketplace with several million "shoppers." In 1994, it staked out a position on the Internet as well, increasing its exposure exponentially.

To convey its message as efficiently as possible, the ANA has established what it calls the Numismatic Information Network—NIN, for short. The association's executive director, Robert J. Leuver, was instrumental in developing this program, having recognized at a very early stage the enormous potential of computer networking.

Through NIN, the ANA posts regularly updated information at its locations on the Internet, CompuServe, and Prodigy. Among other things, it furnishes transcripts of its daily *Money Talks* radio program, as well as press releases and membership information. It also is geared to receive correspondence from its 25,000-plus members, or from the general public. E-mail enables it to expedite requests for library materials, for example—and provides a handy means for prospective new members to seek information and application forms. The ANA's address on the Internet World Wide Web is http://www.money.org.

More and more coin-related "billboards" are appearing along the electronic superhighway and its various byways. My own company, Scott Travers Rare Coin Galleries, Inc. of New York City, has a web site, for example. I use it to provide timely information about the coin marketplace, including significant excerpts from books I have written on rare coins. You can visit the Scott Travers Rare Coin Consumer Protection Home Page at http://www.inch.com/~travers/travers3.htm.

America Online, CompuServe, and Prodigy provide special areas where users can go to obtain information on coin collecting.

- CompuServe has a Collectibles Forum area which includes a section called "Coins/Currency/ANA." This can be accessed by means of GO COINS or GO COLLECTIBLES. "The section offers on-line auctions, nighttime conferences on numismatic topics, and a library from which collectors can download price lists from various dealers," according to prominent coin and collectibles lawyer Armen R. Vartian (CompuServe address 75152-1555), one of the highest-profile members of that area.

- Prodigy has a Collecting Bulletin Board. You can access this by entering JUMP COLLECT, then selecting "Coins & Currency" as the topic.

- America Online has a coin collecting area in its Collector's Corner. To get to it, you GO to the keyword EXCHANGE and then select the Collector's Corner button.

- The USENET Newsgroup is a series of bulletin boards on the Internet. To access the coin collecting bulletin board, go to news: rec.collecting.coins.

Vartian points out that a special feature of CompuServe and Prodigy is their special relationship with ANA (discussed earlier). ANA's education director responds to inquiries in the sections, and information regarding ANA programs often can be found online before it appears in the numismatic press.

CHAPTER 8

HOW YOU CAN MAKE BIG PROFITS FROM SMALL COINS

Many coins rise in value, but often there's great disparity in how much—and how fast—they go up.

You can reap big profits by acquiring the coins with the greatest potential, and in this chapter I show you how to spot these coins quickly and easily. I've put together the ultimate list of secret insider tips—tips available nowhere else in the world—revealing how coin dealers operate and what happens behind the scenes in the marketplace.

Before we go behind the scenes on the sellers' end, let's first take a look at the principal *buyers* of coins and get a better idea how people in general play this money game—how they go about parlaying their small change into big net gains.

For the purposes of our discussion, there are four major groups of people who seek to acquire coins and then put them together—to a greater or lesser extent—systematically: (1) accumulators, (2) collectors, (3) collector/investors, and (4) investors.

Accumulators get their coins out of circulation—from pocket change, at the bank, or possibly in their travels to other countries. The unifying thread is that accumulators don't buy coins; they obtain them for face value.

Collectors, too, look for interesting coins in pocket change. But unlike accumulators, they also *buy* coins—and however they obtain them, they derive great pride and pleasure from assembling their acquisitions into sets. Some collectors purchase coins with million-dollar price tags; others buy coins costing only 50 cents. Whatever the outlay in money or time, true collectors savor the thrill of the hunt. They get much of their satisfaction from *finding* a worthwhile coin—whether that coin is an 1804 silver dollar costing a million dollars or a 1968 Lincoln cent worth only 5 or 10 cents, and whether they find it in pocket change or in a dealer's showcase.

The final two groups of coin buyers we'll consider are collector/investors and investors. These people's interest centers on coins of the highest grade (or level of preservation) and greatest rarity, and in almost every case they acquire them through purchase, rather than discovery. The coin investor looks upon his holdings not so much as a collection, but rather as a portfolio. Nonetheless, the prudent investor acquires and assembles coins systematically. And to maximize his return, he diversifies his holdings, just as he would do with stocks or bonds.

The greatest share of profits has gone to knowledgeable buyers who are either collectors or collector/investors who have studied coins first and who have bought coins based upon their own judgment. A lot of people think that if they send money to an investment advisor in the rare coin field they will make money, but historically this has not been the case.

ACCUMULATORS

Although the accumulator tends to be involved with lower-grade and lower-valued coins than either the collector or the investor, there are still many ways that this type of person can—and does—put together coins in an organized manner.

It's possible, for example, to assemble a complete set of Lincoln Memorial cents by date—or even date and mint mark—from coins found routinely in pocket change. The earlier Lincoln cents with the "wheat-ears" design on the reverse have largely disappeared from circulation, but a good cross-section of Lincoln Memorial cents can still be found, going all the way back to 1959, the year they were introduced. Not being as deeply committed to the hobby as the collector, the typical accumulator probably would be satisfied to acquire just one Lincoln Memorial cent of every date, from 1959 to the present, without going on to consider mint marks, as well.

Jefferson nickels would be another good series for the accumulator. These coins have been issued continuously since 1938 without a significant change in design, and many early dates turn up quite routinely in pocket change. Again, the accumulator would probably be content to save just one coin from every year, rather than seeking one coin from every date and mint. That would greatly improve the odds of being able to find a complete set in circulation. The toughest pieces to locate would probably be the "war nickels" minted from 1942 to 1945. Nickel was urgently needed for war-related purposes during those years, so five-cent pieces were made from a substitute alloy—and silver was used in that alloy. Most of these coins have been pulled out of circulation because their silver content gives them premium value. However, they do show up from time to time.

Yet another goal for the accumulator would be to assemble sets of "clad" Roosevelt dimes and Washington quarters—those produced since 1965, without any silver content. As with war nickels, the earlier dimes and quarters have been saved because their silver makes them worth more as metal than as money. No similar reason exists for saving the later coins, so with a little searching these can be found for every date. It might take time; it might be necessary to go to the bank, obtain some rolls and look through them. But all these coins can be found, at least by date.

Frequently, people accumulate the coins of other nations when they take international trips. They bring these coins home, put them in little envelopes or perhaps a special album, and treat them as mementos of their travels.

Sometimes coin accumulations end up being very much like collections. An accumulator would verge on becoming a collector, for example, if she started saving coins with similar themes—coins depicting animals, for example, or coins portraying ships, or possibly coins that were issued by a number of different countries for Olympic Games.

People who collect very expensive coins believe that the value of individual coins is enhanced by assembling them into sets—that the whole, so to speak, is worth more than the sum of its parts. The truth of this has been demonstrated on numerous occasions when exceptional collections have been offered for sale: Their completeness has resulted in substantially higher premiums. There's no reason why this shouldn't apply, as well, to casual accumulations. And whatever the dollars-and-cents value of such an accumulation, there's no doubt at all that the more time and effort someone invests in coins, the more emotional reward he will gain.

COLLECTORS

Collectors place heavy emphasis on completeness—much more so than accumulators do. While accumulators might be satisfied with a date set of Lincoln Memorial cents, for example, collectors would be more inclined to put together a set with not only every date but also every mint-mark variety. And they might very well extend the set back to the start of the whole Lincoln series in 1909. Such a set would require more time and effort, not to mention more expense, but true collectors have this dedication.

Often, collectors assemble sets of coins according to die varieties. Dies are pieces of steel that impart the design to a coin. You might think of them as cookie cutters. Or picture a rubber stamp and a piece of paper: The stamp corresponds to the die and the piece of paper represents the planchet—the metal blank struck by the die. Different sets of dies may vary somewhat in certain details; perhaps the date is slanted on some or the mint mark is slightly larger. The coins that result can then be differentiated, and collected, according to these varieties. Many collectors put together sets by date, mint mark, *and* die variety.

One of the great attractions of coin collecting is the diversity it provides. Coin collectors can—and do—pursue their hobby in almost innumerable ways. Some collect coins by metal, seeking to acquire a representative example of each coin struck in a specific type of metal, such as silver or gold. Others specialize in particular denominations (silver dollars, for instance) or series (Lincoln cents, perhaps) or time period (such as the twentieth century). And, as noted earlier, collecting coins by themes is another very popular approach—and this offers limitless possibilities. The theme can be broad and general, such as animals, ships, or monarchs. Or it can be quite narrow: I know of several collectors who specialize in coins that depict men or women wearing glasses.

More and more collectors have turned in recent years from date-and-mint collecting to a broader kind of approach in which they collect by *type*. In fact, this may be the single most popular method of collecting coins today. A person who collects by type seeks to obtain a single representative example of each different type of coin—one Lincoln cent, for instance, to represent the whole Lincoln series.

To a great extent, the growing popularity of type collecting reflects the fact that coins have risen in value so spectacularly. Purchasing one example for every date and mint can be prohibitively expensive at current market levels, especially in very high grades, so many collectors content themselves with just one coin from each of the different series.

Since they are acquiring only one coin to represent an entire series, most type collectors want that coin to be a particularly nice one. Thus, they seek the highest-grade piece they can find and can afford. Typically, this will be a common-date coin—since such a coin, of course, would be far more affordable than one of the scarcer and more expensive "keys" in the same high level of preservation. A "key" is a low-mintage, high-value coin. Obtaining one of these is a key to completing the series to which it belongs—hence the name.

Collectors with a great deal of patience and perseverance attempt to assemble "matched" sets of coins. These are sets in which all the coins are exactly the same—or very nearly so—not only in grade but also in appearance. If one coin is toned a certain way, all are toned that way. If one is brilliant and lustrous, so are all the others. It takes time, effort, money, and sometimes a little luck to put together a perfectly matched set, but the final result can be a breathtaking achievement—one that will be a source of enormous satisfaction and potentially significant profit.

COLLECTOR/INVESTORS AND INVESTORS

Collector/investors and investors both are impelled by the profit motive: Making money from coins is important to both these groups. But while the investor looks upon coins as commodities, the collector/investor values them as well for their beauty and historical significance.

The coins with the best track records as money-makers are those with the lowest mintages and those in the highest levels of preservation—in other words, those with the greatest rarity and quality. If profit potential is paramount in *your* scheme of things, you ought to be seeking coins that exist in the fewest numbers or that have the fewest flaws—those which haven't passed from hand to hand and betray few nicks and scratches. If you enjoy a challenge and have a well-padded wallet, you might go after coins with *both* these attributes—those which are both rare *and* well preserved.

Investors tend to favor high-grade examples of common-date coins. These coins are said to be "generic," because even though their dates and mint marks may be different, they resemble each other closely in appearance and value. Generic coins exist in significant numbers, even in high grades such as Mint State-65.

To a far greater extent than the investor, the collector/ investor is interested in completeness. She shares the collector's impulse to start and finish a set. The collector/ investor is a healthy, vibrant breed—one that we're seeing more and more today as the coin business grows into a thriving, bustling multibillion-dollar marketplace.

A lot of coin investors, and even collector/investors, have made mistakes in the past by failing to diversify their holdings. Simply stated, they've put all their eggs in one basket, and all too often the basket has had a hole in it. Perhaps they've heard of a friend or neighbor who made a real killing—a 50-percent profit—on 1881-S Morgan silver dollars, so they've taken all their money and bought up a quantity of 1881-S Morgan dollars graded Mint State-65. But it may have been their misfortune to buy at the top of the cycle, and instead of *making* money, the coins may have decreased in value.

My advice to collector/investors and investors is very simple: Acquire coins by type. For someone with only limited knowledge of coins, this is an excellent way to gain familiarity with the different kinds of coins that are available. It also has the advantage of building in protection against a market decline that hits one kind of coin especially hard. Take the case I just cited, where Morgan dollars suffered a cyclical decline. Chances are that rare-date gold pieces, early type coins, and a number of other coins may not have experienced the same kind of setback, and may have even held their own or gone up. A portfolio containing *all* these different coins would be much more likely to weather any storm and stay on an even keel.

When you collect or invest in coins by type, you're basically getting one representative example of each major kind of United States coin that was struck for people to spend. This can be extremely educational—and never underestimate the importance of education in helping you manage an investment. It also can deepen your aesthetic appreciation for U.S. coinage and stimulate your interest in pursuing one or more areas in greater depth—including certain areas you may not have thought about before, if you were aware of them at all.

SECRET TIPS TO HELP YOU MAKE MONEY

Whether you're a collector, an investor, an accumulator, or a combination of some of these, you can profit greatly from inside knowledge. With this in mind, I'm going to share some tips with you—some secret tips—and offer some valuable insights on how coin dealers operate. I've gleaned this information from years as a market insider and, to the best of my knowledge, it isn't available anywhere else except in this book.

The following information doesn't apply to every single dealer, but it does apply to *some*—even *many*. It's up to you to determine which dealers it applies to and which it doesn't apply to—and that's really a matter of using your common sense.

Dealers have an uneven knowledge of coins. Many dealers are specialists in certain areas, and their in-depth knowledge is limited to the one or two certain areas in which they specialize. If they deal in silver dollars and you bring them some Buffalo nickels for an appraisal, they're really not going to know the Buffalo nickel series that well. They might have a working knowledge, but not an intimate one. As a result, these dealers often have a tendency to overprice material in areas outside their specialties—areas about which they don't have special knowledge. They're afraid a more knowledgeable buyer may take advantage of them.

This should make you wary of buying coins from these dealers outside their specialties. At the same time, however, it also can present some exceptional opportunities. If you look closely at *all* the coins in these dealers' stock, you frequently can find a scarce die variety—or even one of the valuable varieties described in Chapter Two of this book. Invariably, you will find it among the coins outside the dealer's specialty. And when you do, you can "rip" it—get it at a price considerably cheaper than what you might have to pay a specialist. In fact, you might be able to turn right around and sell it to a specialist at a profit. This is what's known in the trade as "cherry-picking" a dealer's inventory.

A good way to learn about coins, and develop the ability to cherry-pick, is to go to pubic auctions, where many rare coins of all different kinds are sold in a single place in a concentrated period of time. Make notes before each auction as to which coins you feel are valuable and which you believe to be special varieties. Then see what kind of prices these coins bring at the auction, when knowledgeable professionals are bidding on them. If your selections attract unusually spirited bidding and strong prices, you've probably picked some real cherries.

Dealers can't always grade coins consistently. Many dealers are not all that astute at grading coins. They're excellent businesspeople and fine entrepreneurs; they're honest, well-meaning, hard-working people. But many smaller dealers just aren't all that proficient at grading coins.

Don't take it for granted that a dealer *is* proficient at grading unless he happens to be a market insider—a dealer who is employed by one of the leading grading services, for example, or possibly even a dealer who *owns* a grading service.

Again, this creates tremendous opportunities for *you*, assuming that you're willing to take the time and effort to gain and sharpen that edge. You can acquire a good basic knowledge of grading within six months by reading up on the subject, then attending public auctions and examining as many coins as possible. At that point, you might very well be able to spot instances where dealers have graded coins too conservatively. That would enable you to pick up some real bargains. A note of caution: This is sophisticated stuff, and I would recommend that you not risk any sizable sum of money unless and until you're absolutely sure of your ability. And, above all, don't pretend to be an expert unless you really are.

Dealers don't heed their own advice during market cycles. Although they may know better, many dealers tend to get caught up in the ebb and flow of current market activity. Dealers may know in principle that if certain kinds of coins—let's say Morgan dollars—are increasing in value at a frenzied pace, they're probably at or near the top of their market cycle. If they went by the book, they would stand back and say to themselves: "Wait a minute, these coins have increased 100 percent in three weeks. This increase is just too great; it's a speculative frenzy; I don't think it's going to last. What's going to happen when all these people decide to sell their coins and take some profits?"

But dealers are only human, and that makes them prone to common human frailties such as greed. Consequently, some will get greedy and continue to buy these coins for their inventory, even though their better judgment tells them the market cycle is already at the top. And this can be very profitable for *you*. Even at the top of a cycle, many dealers will still let you realize your profit and sell your coins back to them because they think the market's going to go even higher. Conversely, at the bottom of a cycle, you'll have the opportunity in many cases—not all the time, but many times—to buy coins at bargain-basement levels. At the bottom, many dealers fall prey to yet another basic human emotion: despair. They become pessimistic and fail to see the light at the end of the tunnel. The herd mentality infects dealers just as it does any other group, so often they'll give you a chance to buy coins inexpensively at the bottom of a cycle.

Thus, in a surprising number of cases, you can sell at the top, because a number of dealers will continue to buy at the top. And you also can buy at the bottom, because so many dealers don't follow their own advice and buy coins when everyone else is selling.

Dealers borrow money for their coin activities and are caught short if the market falls quickly and without notice. It isn't unusual for the coin market to fall very quickly and without any notice. In fact, that's the way it usually *does* fall. When it does, dealers are often caught short financially. What we notice is that after the market retreats, dealers are temporarily unable to buy any more coins. But this doesn't mean that your coins are now worthless, or worth a great deal less than they were before. It's just an indication of temporary market illiquidity.

Let's say a dealer is willing to pay you $100 for a certain coin on a Friday afternoon—then, on Monday morning, he doesn't want to buy it at *any* price, or offers you only $5. This kind of drop is simply too dramatic, and you should flatly refuse to sell the coin. Use your common sense: Hold out until the cash-flow position of that particular dealer—or perhaps of dealers in general—turns around. My experience has been that if you wait a week or so, the cash flow will improve and you'll be able to sell your coin for a much better price. It may be substantially less than the $100 you were offered on Friday afternoon, but it certainly will be substantially more than the $5 Monday morning offer.

Dealers are your No. 1 source of inside information. One good way to anticipate what may be due to increase in value is to check the price guides and see which coins *haven't* gone up in value for a while. Chances are, some of these coins have been at the bottom of their cycle and now may be ready to move up. And an excellent way to confirm your hunch would be to call a number of different dealers and ask them if they have these coins in stock and whether you can purchase them at the going price. If they *don't* have the coins, or won't let them go at the current market price, you can be pretty sure the supplies are thin—and that would reinforce the likelihood of higher prices soon.

Don't tip your hand, or start speculation, by calling a hundred dealers and asking for one or two particular coins. A better approach would be to ask about a number of different coins—ten or twenty, perhaps—and somewhere in that list include the one or two coins in which you're really interested. If you call a hundred dealers and few of them can provide the coins you want at the going price, that's a sure sign that the coins are ripe for a price increase.

Another tipoff would be if you learned that a certain major dealer has been buying specific coins in significant quantities. Let's say you discover that a mail-order dealer with substantial resources has become an aggressive buyer of high-grade Buffalo nickels. You could logically conclude that this dealer was preparing for a big promotional push on Buffalo nickels. That, of course, would stimulate interest—and heightened interest translates into higher prices. By acting quickly and purchasing high-grade Buffalo nickels yourself *before* the dealer's advertising started to appear, you could put yourself in a position to capitalize on the flurry of new activity. In a sense, you could ride the dealer's coattails.

Prices tend to move quickly during a promotional blitz, rising sharply while the push is on and then falling just as sharply once the campaign is over. Thus, you should view this as a short-term situation. Strike while the iron is hot, then take your profits and celebrate.

Dealers don't use magnifying glasses. Everyone should use a magnifying glass in examining coins—but, quite surprisingly, many dealers don't use a glass all the time. As a result, they sometimes overlook imperfections. This is to your advantage when selling coins to these dealers, but may be to your detriment when you buy. I recommend that you use a 5- or 10-power glass when you look at a coin. And be sure that the magnification and lighting conditions are consistent every time. If possible, coins should be viewed under a pinpoint light source such as a tensor lamp or a halogen lamp. Halogen lamps are becoming increasingly popular in examining proof coins. They enable the viewer to spot small hairline scratches quite readily on these coins.

Dealers are small entrepreneurs with families to support and a need for regular income. A dealer is entitled to a reasonable profit on the coins you buy from him; after all, he's in business to make money. However, I don't recommend that you buy into monthly programs where you give a dealer a set amount of money—say, $100 or $200—every single month to buy you coins. In certain months, there just won't be any great buys available.

Monthly programs are especially inadvisable as a method of acquiring pricier coins. If you're talking about investing 25 or 50 thousand dollars a month, you're far better off to establish a relationship with a dealer and have him call you if a suitable coin becomes available. Otherwise, you're putting too much pressure on the dealer, forcing him to get you something extraordinary when it just might not be available in the marketplace.

Dealers would be happy to take your money each month, in every kind of market, because they have families to support and they need a steady income. But that wouldn't always be best from *your* standpoint.

Dealers have a vested interest in buying coins. If you go to some dealers with a coin worth $1,000 and ask "Hey, what's this worth?" you might be told: "I'll give you $50." Needless to say, these dealers would be all too happy to buy such a coin for $50 and then turn around and sell it at a huge profit. That's why I recommend that you get your coins independently certified—a process I discussed at length in Chapter Seven.

Dealers sometimes handle coins improperly, even leaving fingerprints on the coins. When showing your dealer valuable coins—or *any* coins, for that matter, you should pay close attention and ask him politely not to touch the coins on the obverse or reverse. All too often, some dealers handle coins carelessly, sometimes even dropping them. Don't take for granted that just because someone buys and sells coins for a living, he'll treat your coins with care and pick them up only by the edges. He may *know* the right way to handle coins, but he may not always practice it, especially with regard to someone else's coins.

With certified coins, this really isn't a problem. These coins have been encapsulated in sonically sealed, tamper-resistant holders that protect them from such mishandling. What's more, the grading services will not encapsulate a coin if it has any visible residue on its surface which might cause it to deteriorate at a later date. If a certified coin does deteriorate after being encapsulated, the grading service that certified that coin will buy it back.

Dealers who buy coins in quantity often withdraw their public offers to buy these coins just before major conventions. A number of dealers post "bids" to buy coins that they haven't even seen. They place these bids on computer trading networks that are known as "sight-unseen" systems. If you're selling coins through a sight-unseen system, always check to see if any major coin conventions are taking place or imminent. You can do this by looking in *Coin World* or *Numismatic News*, the two leading weekly coin newspapers; both publish detailed coin show schedules. Dealers often withdraw or lower their bids before a major convention, since they don't want to be locked in at a high level—with an obligation to buy at that level—if the market suddenly plunges at the convention.

The coin market is a thin marketplace; at any given time, there may be no more than half a dozen dealers with bids posted on the sight-unseen trading network for certain rare coin types. If all of them withdraw or lower their bids for those coins at the same time—and this does happen, the sight-unseen bids will be substantially lower.

As a rule, dealers attend conventions from Thursday through Saturday. With that in mind, don't sell your coins on a Friday afternoon if you know there's a major convention taking place. You might get much better prices by waiting till Monday morning, when the dealers return from the show and reinstate their normal sight-unseen bids.

Dealers sell rejects, or "off" coins, to other dealers at prices below the wholesale level. I recommend that you establish a working relationship with one or more dealers and ask them about the deals they may have available. Most dealers have certain coins they're willing to sell at discounted prices, but often they prefer to sell these coins to other dealers. By making your interest known, you can sometimes gain access to such deals.

For instance, a dealer may have a certain coin that's been in his stock for six months, and he may just be tired of seeing it. He may say to himself: "You know, it's not that great a coin. I paid $500 for it, but I'd be willing to sell it to another dealer for $300 just to get rid of it. It's not the nicest coin I've ever seen, so I don't want to sell it to a retail client." If you were able to buy this coin for $300, you might be able to turn around and sell it to somebody else for $350 or $400, so it might be a very good deal for you. You might even find it attractive and decide to keep it yourself. Beauty, after all, is often in the eye of the beholder.

By establishing a good relationship with a dealer, you can put yourself in position to purchase cut-rate coins even before they're offered to other dealers. Remember, you *pay* for the special coins; you pay top dollar for exceptional coins that the dealer *wants* his retail clients to have. So why not cut yourself in on bargain coins when those become available?

Dealers absolutely obey the law and file IRS reports on you if you buy coins for cash. The law requires coin and bullion dealers to file a report with the Internal Revenue Service any time you—or your agent or representative—pay more than $10,000 in cash for coin purchases during a given calendar year. And whether they tell you about them or not, the dealers absolutely do file these reports. Never buy coins for cash; always pay by check. Further details on this subject can be found in Chapter Twelve.

ADVICE FROM A TOUGH LAWYER

The most ferocious lawyer I know is Ronald E. Lasky, a partner in the New London, Connecticut, law firm of Ronald E. Lasky & Associates (tel. 1-860-444-6260). Lasky chases after some of the meanest, most vindictive con-men on the face of the earth. He is scared by nothing and will stop at nothing until his client is made whole (reimbursed for damages).

Based on my discussions with Lasky, I have drawn up a list of suggestions on how to check out a coin dealer before doing business with him. These comments reflect on a very small minority of dealers.

- Know the principals of the firm. Check out their backgrounds and qualifications. You must know with whom you are dealing. Many felons and con-men operate under the guise of legitimate businesses. Call your state Attorney General's Office and the AG's office in the state from which your prospective firm operates. Find out if there have been any complaints about the firm or its principals. Also call the Better Business Bureau.
- Investigate the experience level of the people who buy and sell coins for the firm. Ask about their track record in the industry. For whom have they worked in the past? Did they work for legitimate outfits or boiler-room telemarketers? Get names, detailed information on how long they have been with this company and other companies, and then do your homework.
- Ask any prospective firm to give you—in writing—its policies on subjects such as returns, authenticity guarantees, and buy-backs. Be sure your coins are guaranteed to be as described. Get a written guarantee that you can return all coins within a reasonable period for a full refund. Do not buy any coin sight-unseen except under unique circumstances.

On the subject of buy-backs, Lasky's advice to clients is that any guarantee of a buy-back is worthless. If the fine print of virtually all buy-backs is carefully examined,

you will learn that the dealer is in actuality guarantee-
ing nothing. Moreover, the firm will have to be in business and be solvent in the future for your buy-back to
be anything more than an illusion. Lasky's advice here
is that if it sounds too good to be true, it is.

- Check out the firm's financial standing. Ask for financial statements as well as bank and accounting refer-
ences. Never be impressed with large amounts of money
alone; accounting records can mask a great deal of de-
ception.

- Do business only with firms utilizing third-party grading
services. Many so-called third-party grading services actually are in-house (back-room) grading services utilized
by telemarketers. These so-called services grade the coin
as their telemarketer dictates. Lasky recommends buying
coins certified by the Professional Coin Grading Service
(PCGS), the Numismatic Guaranty Corporation (NGC),
or ANACS.

- Determine whether the firm has had a history of litigation with governmental or other entities. A company
continually incurring sanctions from the Federal Trade
Commission would not be on my list of recommended
firms.

- You should never send your money directly to a coin
firm—especially if the firm is not well known, but
even when dealing with well-known firms which are
on somewhat financially suspect grounds. Rather, use
an escrow agent who will release your funds to the
firm only when you have received your coins. If this
approach is not taken, the firm may disappear with
your money or refuse to send you your coin. As unrea-
sonable as it sounds, Lasky has represented a number
of individuals who have had this happen to them. You

will find that legitimate firms will not object to your use of an escrow agent. Escrow agents are not difficult to locate; for instance, most attorneys have a wealth of experience acting as escrow agents for clients.

Q. David Bowers, chairman of Bowers and Merena Galleries in Wolfeboro, New Hampshire, perhaps the most successful coin dealer of all time, said that he has never had a single client ever put money in escrow. He also said that he has never had a single client who has failed to receive the coins for which he or she has paid. "This might be necessary if you are dealing with some type of telemarketer," Bowers stated. "But I don't think you are recommending that people do this."

- Never permit the coin firm to store your coins for you. Always take physical possession. Failure to do so could embroil you in needless litigation should a third party claim your coin as his.

Rare coin investments can be both enjoyable and extremely profitable if you follow the Golden Rule in selecting a firm: Check it out!

SUMMING UP

Unlike any other investment field, the rare coin market produces only winners. This isn't to say that coins don't go down in value; certainly, coins go down—sometimes they decrease quickly and by a big percentage. But coins are so beautiful that even if some of your coins fail to appreciate monetarily, you still come out ahead because you get *aesthetic* appreciation.

Of course, you would prefer to gain *both* types of

appreciation, and that's where *One-Minute Coin Expert* comes in. By following the guidelines and using the secret tips I've given you in this chapter, you'll have a big head start in picking coins with the potential to realize tremendous gains.

CHAPTER 9

HOW TO CASH IN THOSE BIG PROFITS

Congratulations! You've looked in the cookie jar, searched the attic, checked your pocket change—and now you're ready to go to the cash window and celebrate. You've found some coins that are valuable, other coins that are extremely valuable, and still other coins that may even be super-rarities.

Maybe you've discovered a circulated 1932 double eagle ($20 gold piece) worth $5,000. Or possibly you've come up with a circulated 1797 Draped Bust half dollar with 15 stars on the front, which is worth a tidy $18,500. These coins are easy enough to sell; dealers all over the nation want to buy them. I'll provide you with details later in this chapter on how to sell them.

But suppose you've really struck it rich. Suppose, for instance, you've found a circulated 1870-S three-dollar gold piece worth half a million dollars. It's easy enough to sell this coin, too. But it's not quite so simple to obtain the full value for a coin in this rarefied price range. You may have dealers across the country beating a path to your door and wanting to buy it for $300,000. You may even find a couple of dealers willing to buy it for $400,000. But if you want to sell it for its full value, you may have to wait a little while—or even longer—in order to maximize what you can sell it for.

Generally, the higher the price you ask for your 1870-S three-dollar gold piece, or any other extremely valuable coin, the longer you'll have to wait for a buyer. But this is not unique to rare coins. It's much like what you would encounter, for example, if you tried to sell your house.

A friend of mine owned a house in New Jersey, where the real estate market was depressed at the time. He decided to move with his family to a different part of the state, and he foolishly bought a house there without first making sure to sell his first house. He was confident he could sell it with no problem at all if he simply lowered the price somewhat.

Surprise! Many months elapsed without a single offer on the old house, leaving my friend in a major cash-flow bind since he needed the proceeds from that house to help finance the new one.

Big-ticket coins are sometimes very much like real estate. If you own a coin for which you paid $100,000, selling it may not be as quick and easy a deal as you might think. You can't simply take it to any of a thousand willing dealers, all of whom have $100,000 in cash on hand and are pleading with you to let them buy that coin.

Selling your extremely valuable coins is similar to selling your house. You might be able to sell that coin, or that piece of real estate, almost instantaneously; maybe you'll simply get lucky. In most cases, though, especially in instances where the coin is worth a whole lot of money, the process of selling is a much longer one and one which requires some planning and some good, quick-witted common sense on your part.

A few years ago, a rare and beautiful United States gold coin was sold for more than $1.5 million. The coin is an "ultra-high-relief" 1907 double eagle, or $20 gold piece, designed by renowned sculptor Augustus Saint-Gaudens. This coin was graded Mint State-68 on the 1-through-70 scale by the Numismatic Guaranty Corporation.

This probably was not an instantaneous sale; this was not a spur-of-the-moment transaction where a coin dealer had the coin in his hip pocket and said to himself, "You know, I think I might want to sell this coin because I need the money." This wasn't a situation where he just went out and walked up to someone who said, "I'll give you a million-and-a-half for it," and then the coin dealer said "okay" and the buyer took $1.5 million out of his back pocket and put the money on the table.

Transactions such as this involve detailed negotiations— frequently extended ones. They're planned far ahead of time and the people selling these coins give careful consideration to psychological factors in the marketplace.

Financial service professionals regard stocks as being "continuously liquid." At any given time, you can take a share of stock and sell it for the price that's published in the newspaper or the current trading price of that stock— and for every share you sell, you'll receive a uniform price. At any given time, that stock is salable.

To a certain extent, some coins which are not great rarities enjoy this same advantage. We often see $1,000 coins and $500 coins and $100 coins which, for all practical purposes, are continuously liquid. But when we start talking about large groups of these coins, or coins which have fancy price tags, these coins lack continuity of liquidity. These coins are not always readily salable at any given time.

Let's say a dealer has three boxes of coins and he takes them to a show, figuring he can sell them under current market conditions for $2 million. But when he gets to the show, where many other dealers have a chance to examine the coins, the best offer he gets is only $1 million. Chances are that dealer wouldn't sell those coins. He would wait until the next show, figuring he would get a better offer. He might have to wait a month to find the right buyer, the person willing to pay $2 million—or close to $2 million—for those coins, but the difference in price would make the wait worthwhile.

In this case and other cases like it, the "right buyer" is the person who:

- *Needs the coin*—a dealer who needs it to sell to a collector; a collector who needs it to complete a collection; a collector-investor who needs it for a type set.
- *Appreciates the coin*—someone who appreciates its cultural, artistic, or historical significance; someone who appreciates its rarity; someone who appreciates its high grade; someone who likes the design of this kind of coin; someone who finds the toning unusually attractive.
- *Has the money to pay for the coin*—someone who can pay for it within a reasonable time.

If someone is buying a coin for a million dollars, he can't be expected to pay for it tomorrow. And if he is able to pay for it tomorrow, he, in turn, will expect the seller to extend advantageous terms. If he can pay for it within a month or two, that's fine. When I speak of someone who can pay for the coin, I don't necessarily mean a dealer with the money in his hip pocket. It could instead be a dealer who knows a private collector who wants that particular coin, or a dealer who can secure the proper financing. This ability, coupled with his own financial resources, would enable him to give you the best possible price for the coin you're selling.

Unless all three of these factors are involved, there won't be any sale.

This is really no different from what you would encounter in trying to sell a house. Unless you were lucky enough to find the right buyer—someone who needed your house, appreciated your house, and had the money to buy it—you wouldn't be able to swap your "For Sale" sign for one reading "Sold."

THE MONEY SUPPLY

The coin market's money supply is governed by four basic factors: cash flow, debt payments, bank collateral, and market fluctuations.

Cash flow is the two-way pattern of payments: money received by a dealer and money spent. If a dealer sells a coin for $1,000 but doesn't get paid by his client for thirty days—even though the dealer had to pay for the coin right away, that dealer may very well have a cash-flow problem. This type of negative cash flow, multiplied by a number of different deals, could have a significant impact on that coin dealer's ability to pay a strong price for your coins at any given time.

Just about everyone has *debt payments*, and coin dealers are certainly no exception. Dealers who maintain coin shops often have heavy debts, including mortgage payments and installment-loan payments on expensive computer equipment. These debts can sometimes limit their ability to wheel and deal freely in buying and selling coins.

Many dealers also are repaying loans for which they have used coins as *bank collateral*. When the market goes down, many dealers in a sense "hock" some of their coins in order to obtain needed cash. In the late 1980s a dealer might have taken $500,000 worth of coins to the Safra-Bank of California, or some other institution offering such a service, and been able to obtain a loan for 50 percent—or sometimes as much as 70 percent—of the coins' value, based on the current sight-unseen prices on the computerized trading network. Some banks still offer such loans.

Dealers have to make payments on such loans—and if coin prices go down further, they have to come up with more coins (or other assets) to keep the value of their collateral at 50 or 70 percent of their loan balance. Otherwise, they have to repay the money. Thus, a declining market can place a particular strain on dealers using coins as collateral—and, in the process, magnify the weakness of the money supply in the marketplace as a whole.

Market fluctuations can never be predicted with pinpoint accuracy, but they certainly play a role in determining how much—or how little—money will be available. Dealers' profits are maximized in a rising market, and that in turn gives them more money to spend on buying coins.

SALES OPTIONS

There are three primary methods by which you can sell your coins: direct sale, electronic trading networks, and public auctions.

Direct sale is a highly personalized, specialized area which won't be covered in great detail in this book because it involves such subjectivity—such interpersonal chemistry between the seller and buyer. I don't recommend the direct sale approach because in many cases, the person buying the coins has a vested interest in the outcome of the transaction.

The buyer might say your coins are worth nothing when, in fact, they're really worth thousands—or even millions—of dollars. That's why third-party certification is so important. If you have coins and you don't know what they're worth, you should get them independently certified before you attempt to sell them.

Electronic Trading The principal network through which you can sell your coins electronically is the Certified Coin Exchange (CCE). You'll have to get your coins certified beforehand by one of the two leading coin-grading services.

The Certified Coin Exchange accepts coins certified by either the Professional Coin Grading Service (PCGS) or the Numismatic Guaranty Corporation of America (NGC).

To use this trading option, you'll need to have a dealer submit your coins to NGC or PCGS. Both firms will be happy to provide you with a free list of member dealers. You'll find these dealers extremely helpful. Once your coins are certified, the dealer you select will help you again in determining the current sight-unseen bids. Just ask him to show you the computer screen or a printout of the current high bids. Chances are, the dealer will charge a commission of 10 or 15 percent to handle the sale for you. And that is certainly fair and reasonable.

The electronic exchanges will be of greatest use to you in selling coins that are fungible—high-grade examples of common-date coins that resemble each other in appearance and value and thus are interchangeable. These coins are said to be commoditized, and they lend themselves readily to sight-unseen trading, especially when they trade for less than $250 apiece.

As I explained earlier, these coins are continuously liquid for all practical purposes—unless you have several million dollars' worth that you want to dump at one time. The coin market has a number of small entrepreneurs, and if you try to sell several million dollars' worth of anything, it's not going to be as easy as selling a smaller quantity with a lower market value. You could certainly do it; a transaction in the millions could certainly be consummated. But it probably would take a lot more time and effort.

Auction Sales Auction sales offer some highly significant advantages to you as a seller, and I happen to like this particular option very much. These sales bring many prospective buyers together in one place, and that can produce competitive bidding that will drive up the prices you receive.

In a conventional auction, your coins are showcased in a beautiful catalog, where they are described very attractively—and possibly pictured, as well. This helps produce a sort of mystique, a sense that the auction coins are special. And that, in turn, enhances the prices they realize.

Conventional auctions do have a downside, however. First and foremost is the fact that substantial time will pass between when you consign the coins and when you receive your money. Typically, it takes about two to three months for coins to come under the gavel after they're submitted to an auction company for sale in the conventional manner. Then, after the auction, another thirty to forty-five days will pass before you receive your money.

Clearly, the time lag involves a serious risk. Let's say you consign some coins to an auction house in January and they don't come up for sale until March. If the coin market experienced a cyclical decline and your coins went down in value 10 or 20 percent from January to March, you would receive a lower return. And this kind of cyclical decline isn't uncommon. There are ways to protect your coins from selling at auction for unacceptably low prices, and I'll discuss these shortly. However, there's no way to force bidders to pay January prices in March when the March prices are lower, and you should keep this in mind when deciding whether to sell your coins at auction.

The growing volatility in the marketplace has increased the possibility that coins could go down in value after being consigned for public auction. This has given rise to a quick and easy new method of selling coins at auction. One company calls this method the "express auction." Another calls it the "bullet auction." Whatever the name, it's a method that greatly reduces the delay of the conventional auction route.

Suppose you have a coin whose value has risen 200 percent since you acquired it and you want to cash out and take your profit. At the same time, however, you want to be sure of getting the highest price, and you feel the best way to do that is to sell the coin at auction. By consigning the coin to a company that conducts express—or bullet—auctions, you can benefit from the competitive bidding atmosphere of a public auction without enduring the worrisome lag time often inherent in old-style auction sales. There's a good chance your coin can be sold at one of the new, quicker auctions within a few weeks. And the payment will be quicker, too. Companies conducting express auctions require faster payment from successful bidders, and they in turn then pay their consignors almost at once.

This type of auction is becoming an extremely viable alternative. And besides saving you time, it can also save you money. That's because express or bullet auctions tend to be "no-frills" sales, creating substantial savings which then can be passed along. The catalogs for these auctions can't be as elaborate, for example, because of the limited time; they can't make lavish use of full-color illustrations as conventional auction catalogs often do. Because of such economies, the commission you'll have to pay is likely to be significantly lower than at a traditional auction house.

Market secret: If you decide to sell your coins by means of an express or bullet auction, consign them only to a company that also conducts the more elaborate, more traditional kind. These full-service companies have built up large mailing lists and enjoy the patronage of many thousands of clients to whom they can send catalogs for their sales, including the quicker auctions. If a "fly-by-night" firm were to set up one of these quickie auctions, you wouldn't get good results in many cases.

HOW TO PROTECT YOURSELF WHEN YOU SELL A COIN AT AUCTION

There are three potential risks in buying and selling coins.

Probably first and foremost is the *buy risk*—the risk that what you get will be less than what you paid for. As long as you limit your purchases to coins that have been certified, the buy risk will be greatly minimized or even eliminated.

Then there is the *market risk*—the risk that if you buy a coin, instead of going up by 300 percent it might go down a couple of percentage points.

Finally, you have the *sell risk*—the risk that when you dispose of your coins, the payment you receive will be less than what they're worth. To use an extreme example, you might have coins worth $100,000 and some unscrupulous dealer might offer you only $50. If you were naive enough to sell them for $50, the dealer would then go out and sell those coins for their true value and reap the enormous dividend that rightfully should have been yours.

Selling your less expensive coins at auction isn't like selling real estate by the same sales route. Houses and other pieces of real estate often change hands at auction for substantially less than their normal market value— what they would bring if their owners had time to sit tight and wait for the right buyer, the buyer with the combination of ingredients I outlined earlier in this chapter. Desirable coins tend to bring strong prices when sold at auction; there's great competition for these coins.

Sometimes, an auction company will agree to take raw coins—coins that have not been certified—and describe them optimistically in its catalog. This would make these coins appear to be in a higher grade than they actually are. In a sense, this is not unlike what a used car dealer does when he takes a car that's a lemon, represents it to be a cream puff, and sells it on someone's behalf to an unsuspecting consumer. An auction company might be willing to do this on your behalf—so before consigning your coins for sale in the company's auction, you should first ask what grade it intends to assign to each coin.

If the auction company doesn't want to grade your coins in accordance with your wishes, I recommend that you have them independently certified before consigning them. This would establish their actual grade beyond any reasonable doubt. They might not then be graded optimistically in the catalog, but they also wouldn't be given too low a grade. Be sure to have your coins certified only by leading grading services.

Any time you sell your coins, you should seek to take advantage of market trends; in other words, you should try to anticipate upward movements and time your auction consignments so the coins' sale coincides closely with a cycle's high. This, of course, is easier said than done, and even the experts guess wrong now and then.

To protect yourself against the possibility that you may be guessing wrong, and that the market may actually decline before your coins come up for sale, you should work out an arrangement with the auction house beforehand to assign a "reserve" value to each of your coins. If the bidding fails to reach this level, you will then get to keep the coins. You may have to pay a commission on the reserve price, but at least your coins won't be sold for less than they're worth.

The traditional, or three-month, auction route is best suited to coins that are real rarities. These coins need the exposure they receive in fancy catalogs and extensive promotional buildups. Elaborate trappings aren't really "frills" when it comes to great rarities, since it takes this kind of approach to attract the right kind of buyer for such coins.

If you have commodity-type coins such as common-date Morgan dollars graded Mint State-65, you can place these in bullet sales or sell them through the electronic exchanges.

If you have coins that fall somewhere in between, such as beautiful Mint State-65 or Proof-65 Liberty Seated quarters that are worth perhaps $2,000 each, you certainly could consign them to a bullet sale. But these coins should not be sold over the electronic exchanges. Each of these coins has an idiosyncratic quality of toning, of appearance, and the electronic exchanges tend to minimize, rather than maximize, special qualities. These exchanges emphasize the *similarities* that certain coins possess, not their *differences*—and beautiful toning can be a very positive difference that makes a coin more valuable than the norm.

Competition is healthy for sellers; when selling your coins, you want as many buyers as possible competing to purchase them. At an auction, the competition is already built in: The gallery will be filled with people who are vying for your coins. But if for some reason you don't want to sell a coin at auction, you still can stimulate strong competition for that coin—and get the highest price possible—by showing it to twelve or fifteen different dealers and having each one give you a sealed bid. This isn't nearly as effective as the public auction route, but it's better than going to just one dealer and being at his mercy.

Selling your coins can be a pleasurable and profitable experience. Just remember that some coins can be sold more readily than others, and all coins can be sold more readily at certain times than at other times. You can sell a million-dollar coin instantaneously, but you may get only $800,000 for that coin.

With super-rarities, if you want to maximize the amount of money you get, you may have to wait a little while. With coins valued at $10,000—and even $20,000 or $30,000, you can get full value almost immediately.

CHAPTER 10

SCOTT TRAVERS'
SECRET TOP TEN

Coins that have great potential to rise in value sharply, but aren't yet performing at close to their potential, are said to be *sleepers*.

Sleepers can be found among certified coins—coins that have been examined, graded, and encapsulated by one of the leading grading services. They also can be found among "raw" coins—coins that haven't yet been certified and encased (or "slabbed") in sonically sealed, hard plastic holders.

Some sleepers have greater potential than others. In this chapter, I reveal a secret list of ten coins, or types of coins, which are among the biggest sleepers of all—the very best buys—in the current marketplace.

If you have money to spend on rare coins, these are potential purchases that merit your serious consideration, since all are excellent values.

You may not have to buy some of these coins; it's certainly possible to find any or all of them in an old collection or accumulation that may be sitting right now in a drawer or cigar box in your home.

Recently, I performed an appraisal for people who had come into possession of just such a group of rare coins. The people who owned these coins thought they had little

or no value—but when I examined them, I found they included a number of rare and valuable pieces, among
them low-mintage proofs. At my suggestion, the owners
got some of them certified; the coins came back from the
grading service with grades as high as Proof-65, making
them worth premiums ranging as high as tens of thousands of dollars per coin.

If you do find some of the coins in my secret list—in
the cookie jar, in the attic, or in an old collection you received as an inheritance—hold on to them. Because of
their great potential, all these coins could rise in value
dramatically in the long run, or even in a much shorter
term. Think twice before selling them; they could bring
you much more substantial returns later on.

If you don't find any of these ten sleepers but are
thinking of investing in coins, these would be excellent
items to buy. I've chosen a cross-section of coins with
current retail prices ranging from modest amounts to six-
figure sums, so you'll find something here for just about
every budget.

In buying them, as in selling them, certification is
highly advisable. "Slabbed" coins—those that have been
certified—enjoy broad popularity and great liquidity in
today's coin market, and by limiting your transactions to
certified coins you will greatly enhance the security of
your investment.

You can buy or sell a number of certified coins sight-
unseen through any of the hundreds of coin dealers
nationwide who are members of the Certified Coin Exchange (CCE). And while prices fluctuate, you can get
a good idea of your coins' current value by referring
to the values in the *Certified Coin Dealer Newsletter* (or
Bluesheet), an authoritative weekly price guide of the

sight-unseen market. This publication is also an excellent indicator of which grading services are in favor at any given time, since it lists market prices only for the services whose coins are most widely traded.

Here, then, is my special ten-coin list:

1. Uncirculated silver clad Eisenhower dollars dated 1973 and 1974.

The Eisenhower dollar was the last U.S. dollar coin of the large, traditional size. This undoubtedly gave it sentimental appeal to some, but many found fault with it for the very same reason that millions of Americans of earlier generations had chosen not to carry "cartwheels" around: They found it inconveniently bulky. To make matters worse, Eisenhower dollars produced for circulation weren't even silver; like other formerly silver coins minted since 1965, they were "clad" coins consisting of an outer layer of copper-nickel metal bonded to a core of pure copper. The uninitiated called them "silver dollars," but this was a misnomer.

First issued in 1971, the Eisenhower dollar was meant as a tribute to former President Dwight D. Eisenhower, who had died two years earlier. Since it came into being during the presidency of Richard M. Nixon, it was widely perceived as having a political basis, as well, in the sense that it provided a "Republican" coin to balance the "Democratic" Kennedy half dollar.

The Eisenhower dollar never caught on with the public and was issued for only eight years before being replaced in 1979 by an even shorter-lived coin: the much smaller Susan B. Anthony dollar. During that brief time, however, numerous collectible Ike-dollar varieties were produced. These tend to be overlooked because the series was so short, so recent, and so unenthusiastically received not only by the populace as a whole but also by many collectors. But a close look suggests that some of these varieties have excellent potential for price appreciation at today's depressed market levels.

I am particularly bullish on the silver clad Ike dollars of 1973 and 1974. A word of explanation is in order: Although the dollars struck for circulation contained no precious metal, the U.S. Mint did produce limited quantities of these coins in silver clad composition for sale to collectors at a premium. Like the Kennedy halves of 1965 through 1970, these coins had a silver content of 40 percent—well below the pre-1965 level of 90 percent, but silver nonetheless.

The Mint offered silver clad Ike dollars individually from 1971 through 1974 in both proof and uncirculated versions. Each proof came in a bulky brown box and each uncirculated example in a slimmer blue package, prompting dealers and collectors to label these "brown-pack" and "blue-pack" Ikes. At $10 each, the proofs were quite pricey; at $3 apiece, blue-pack Ikes were seen as a better buy. Mintages of both were relatively high in 1971, the first year of issue, but the novelty wore off quickly as demand in the resale market fell far short of supply. By 1973, the Mint received orders for fewer than 1.9 million blue packs, or less than one-third the number it had gotten in 1971, when nearly 6.9 million were sold. Sales rose only slightly in 1974, barely topping 1.9 million.

At one point in the 1980s, blue-pack Ikes from 1973 and 1974 were worth $20 or more on the wholesale level. As this is written, they're selling for a mere $2.50 apiece. That's only about a 50-percent premium over their bullion value, for each contains a little more than three-tenths of an ounce of silver. These are highly promotable coins, and it wouldn't take much promotion to drive their price from $2.50 to $6 or more. Those numbers may be small, compared with the fancy premiums commanded by truly rare coins, but percentagewise such an increase would be enormous.

I don't regard blue-pack Ikes as a long-term investment; this is a gimmicky area, and you should regard it as more of a speculation. But it's certainly an interesting play—and if you have $50 or even $100 to spare, it might very well enable you to double that money within a very short time. These are extremely affordable coins, they're more than twenty years old, their mintages are modest, their bullion value is significant relative to their cost—and if the price of silver were to rise dramatically, these coins would become all the more promotable and all the more valuable intrinsically.

2. Proof war nickels.

Production of U.S. proof coins was halted by the Mint during World War II. Prior to the suspension, though, the Mint did produce a proof version of one "war nickel": the five-cent emergency issue made at the main mint in Philadelphia in 1942. This coin has a large "P" above Monticello's dome. (*Note:* Prior to removing nickel from the coin, the Mint also made proof 1942 Jefferson five-cent pieces of the standard copper-nickel composition. To be sure your coin is a war nickel proof, check for the "P" above the dome.)

In Proof-65, a 1942-P war nickel certified by an independent grading service would cost you only about $75 sight-unseen. An extra-nice specimen actually seen before purchase would cost perhaps $350. These are sensational values.

These coins contain silver. They're quite scarce, with a mintage of only 27,600, and a lot of them have deteriorated, making the survivors even scarcer. They're novel—the only proof examples of the war nickel type. Noncollectors appreciate them because of their uniqueness. And, best of all, they're reasonably priced.

Besides being great values, they're also marvelous conversation pieces—something you can keep around the house and impress your friends with. People are fascinated when they see a "nickel" coin made of silver. And because of their unparalleled quality, proof coins showcase this difference best of all.

3. 1890-O Morgan silver dollars graded Mint State-64.

My third recommendation is the 1890 Morgan silver dollar from the New Orleans Mint. This coin can be identified by the "O" (for New Orleans) mint mark, which appears just below the eagle, near the base of the reverse.

The 1890-O Morgan dollar is characterized by a weak strike: On most examples of this coin, the details of the design were softly defined, not razor sharp, even on the day they left the mint. Often, this makes even nice Mint State specimens appear to be in a lower grade than they actually are. This, in turn, makes grading these coins rather tricky, even for the professionals at the coin grading services.

Independent grading services have assigned a
grade of Mint State-64 to many 1890-O Morgan dollars which are, in fact, almost the equivalent of Mint
State-65. In some cases, they actually are Mint State-
65 but have slipped through at the lower grade because their weak strike was so deceptive. These are
often very attractive coins, perhaps with light russet-
golden toning and maybe just a minor nick or two.

In Mint State-64, the current price of an 1890-O
dollar certified by one of the leading independent grading services is $130 sight-unseen. A super premium-
quality Mint State-64 example, one that looks like a
Mint State-65, would cost $200 at most. But if the
same coin were certified as Mint State-65, it would
cost about $1,300. And the difference in appearance
is frequently almost negligible. To the naked eye, in
fact, some 1890-O dollars graded Mint State-65 aren't
nearly as attractive as some of their Mint State-64
counterparts.

You'll often find one of these coins properly certified as Mint State-65 because it's free from marks—
yet its toning may be rather unattractive and its strike
may very well be incomplete. In a holder from a
leading independent grading service, this coin will
sell for thousands of dollars. Its Mint State-64 counterpart could be nearly fully struck and have beautiful toning, but fall just short of Mint State-65
because of a tiny mark or two. This Mint State-64
coin probably would cost you less than one-tenth the
price of the Mint State-65, yet it would be more sat-
isfying to own.

Quite possibly, you might even be able to get the
coin certified as Mint State-65 by removing it from

its Mint State-64 holder and resubmitting it to one of the leading grading services. Borderline coins—coins which might be assigned either of two different grades—are, in fact, assigned different grades at different times. If you were able to buy an 1890-O dollar graded Mint State-64 for $130, or even $200, and then got it recertified as Mint State-65, you would be able to sell it for five times or more what you paid for it.

This is just one of many instances where the difference in price between Mint State-64 and Mint State-65 is many dollars—where the Mint State-64 coin has a rather inexpensive price tag and its Mint State-65 counterpart is priced prohibitively. Many of these Mint State-64 coins represent good values. But in buying them, you should be certain not to pay an excessive amount for premium-quality pieces. If the going price is $250 in Mint State-64 and $2,000 in Mint State-65, clearly $800 or $1,000 would be too much to pay for a premium-quality Mint State-64 example. But $400 sounds just right.

4. Trade dollars graded Proof-63 or Proof-64.

After the Civil War, the U.S. government turned its attention abroad and sought to expand its trade with foreign nations. As part of this effort, Congress created a new silver coin called the Trade dollar. This coin was similar in size and appearance to the regular silver dollar, but contained a bit more silver. It was meant for use in the Orient, where merchants preferred to be paid with precious-metal coins.

The Trade dollar was a short-lived and essentially unsuccessful innovation: It remained in production for little more than a decade, from 1873 to 1885, and during the last seven years it was minted only in proof form, for sale at a premium to the public. However, it's a high-priced and highly prized collectible.

Trade dollars graded Proof-63 and Proof-64 are sleepers. Once again, there's a gap between the market prices in Proof-64 and Proof-65. As this is written, a Proof-64 example has a fair market retail value of $2,000, while a Proof-65 is worth $5,000. And the difference in appearance between these two coins is very slight.

I especially like Proof-63 Trade dollars. These are priced right now at only about $1,400 each—and like their Proof-64 counterparts, many appear quite similar to Proof-65 pieces when viewed with the unaided eye. You can get a coin that's virtually identical to a Proof-65 except for a couple of hairlines. And buyers have a tendency to overlook those minuscule hairlines when viewing a coin with great aesthetic appeal. You're getting a coin with almost the same eye appeal for only about one fifth the price.

Look for a Proof-63 Trade dollar with dramatic contrast between its snow-white devices (the raised portions of the design) and its chromium-like fields (the flat background areas). You might have to pay a somewhat higher price than you would for an ordinary Proof-63, but the extra cost would be money well spent. That type of stunning cameo contrast would make such a coin tremendously appealing to most people who saw it, and they'd probably disregard the hairlines that reduced its technical grade.

Be on the lookout for Trade dollars which have been certified as Proof-63 by one of the leading independent grading services. Many of these coins can be taken out of their holders and sold at a later time for a higher price. I've seen many dealers do just that: They'll buy a certified Proof-63 Trade dollar at a convention for the going price—let's say $1,200—and then take it out of its "slab" and sell it immediately at the same convention for $3,000 to $4,000 to another dealer who thinks that he can get it certified as Proof-65.

Caution: Be careful in purchasing "raw" (or uncertified) proof Trade dollars. Many of these coins have been certified and encapsulated and then removed from their plastic holders because their owners felt the assigned grades were too low. You may be misled into grading such a coin optimistically and thus paying too much for it.

5. **Proof-64 Variety 3 Liberty Head double eagles (1877–1907).**

The double eagle, or $20 gold piece, is the largest gold coin the U.S. Mint ever made for use in commerce. Each of these coins contains nearly one full ounce of gold, giving it a value of several hundred dollars just as metal. But many double eagles are much more than merely pieces of metal: They're beautiful, desirable collectibles that often command premiums of tens, or even hundreds, of thousands of dollars.

The double eagle made its first appearance in 1849, so it is, quite literally, a "Forty-Niner." It was, in fact, the California Gold Rush that gave rise to the issuance of this coin. It remained an important part of U.S. coinage for more than eighty years before being discontinued in 1933, at a time when Americans were mired in the Great Depression.

The first double eagle produced by the Mint is known as the Coronet or Liberty Head type because its design depicts a crowned figure of Liberty. This type, in turn, is divided into three different varieties because of small but important differences in the inscriptions. Double eagles minted from 1877 to 1907 are denoted as Variety 3 because they bear the inscription *IN GOD WE TRUST* and have the words *TWENTY DOLLARS* spelled out at the base of the reverse.

Very few proof double eagles were produced: In most years, the total proof mintage was less than one hundred. Proof-64 examples of the Variety 3 Liberty Head double eagle are almost unknown—yet they can be acquired for about $21,000 each. This sounds like a lot of money, and it is. But it's really quite a bargain—in fact, it's an absolutely phenomenal value—because these coins are so rare and so desirable. In Proof-66, the same coin would probably cost upwards of $75,000, and there's really little difference in the way the two coins look.

In buying proof double eagles, acquire only coins with cameo contrast—that is, a strong contrast between the devices (the raised portions of the design) and the fields (the flat background areas). Ideally, the devices should be frosted and the fields should have a lovely mirrorlike sheen.

You can expect cameo proofs to cost a little more than regular ones; they generally sell for 10 to 15 percent, or even 20 percent, above the cost of their counterparts without the cameo contrast. But the difference in price is negligible compared with the increased value this eye-catching feature will impart to your spectacular coin.

Double eagles are very large coins with exceptional appeal to noncollectors. Never underestimate the importance of size as a selling point with such buyers. Investors are smitten with large, bold-looking coins—especially when they're made from gold or silver. That's why silver dollars are so popular with investors, and double eagles enjoy the same kind of popularity.

As the coin market expands and more and more noncollectors enter the field, interest in coins such as proof double eagles will almost surely grow by leaps and bounds. Many of these newcomers will have large sums of money to spend, and many will be drawn to big, beautiful coins made of gold and silver.

The Proof-64 Variety 3 Liberty double eagle is rare. Its aesthetic appeal is awesome. And it has a rock-solid collector base. Add up all these elements and what you have is a coin with almost unlimited potential. We may very well see this coin command a six-figure price tag in the not-too-distant future if the coin market expands as I expect it to.

6. **Mint State-65 and Proof-65 copper coins.**

Copper coins in general, just about across the board, are really exceptional sleepers. These coins didn't participate to any great extent in the market's spectacular boom of the late 1970s and early 1980s, and while major copper rarities have certainly risen in value over the years, their growth has been far more limited than that of similar coins in gold and silver.

The reasons for this are partly physical and partly psychological. Copper coins are susceptible to unsightly—and irreversible—discoloration, and this can cause permanent impairment of their surfaces and substantial reduction in their value. Damage of this type can be averted with proper precautions, but instead of being familiarized with the precautions, investors have been systematically discouraged over the years from even considering copper coins. This has created a deep-seated bias against these coins in many buyers' minds.

Concern is certainly warranted, but blind rejection of all copper coins is an overreaction. Besides closing their minds, investors who harbor this prejudice are also closing the door to profits that are potentially very sizable.

Matte-proof Lincoln cents were made by the U.S. Mint from 1909 to 1916. Their surfaces have a dull, almost sandblasted type of look, very unlike the mirrorlike appearance of most other U.S. proof coins. Identifying these proofs can be tricky for the uninitiated, so I advise you to buy only coins that have been certified. In grading these coins, and copper coins in general, independent grading services distinguish between those that are fully original in color (certified as "RD" for "Red"), those that have some original color but also some toning (certified as "RB" for "Red and Brown") and those that are fully toned (certified as "BN" for "Brown"). Fully red Proof and Mint State coins are considered the most desirable, but many buyers favor copper coins with toning, since these are less susceptible to possible surface damage.

I particularly like matte-proof Lincoln cents that have been certified by one of the leading independent grading services as Proof-65 RB (Red and Brown). As this is written, these coins can be obtained for just $150, and that's an incredible value. They're extremely underrated and very, very difficult to obtain. At $600, matte-proof Lincolns certified as Proof-65 RD (Red) are also excellent buys. Often, a coin certified as Proof-65 Red and Brown can be resubmitted to a grading service and then will be assigned a new grade of Proof-65 Red, effectively almost quadrupling its market value.

Matte-proof Lincolns graded Proof-64 RD (Red) are also very good values. As of this writing, these coins are priced at $250 each, and I consider that a phenomenal bargain. But don't buy a Proof-64 with the idea of resubmitting the coin to an independent grading service in quest of an upgrade to Proof-65. With these particular coins, there's a big difference between 64 and 65 and I don't think you'll be able to buy a Proof-64 RD for $250, resubmit the coin, and get back a Proof-65 RD worth $600. It really doesn't happen in this area. But the Proof-64 still represents a terrific value.

7. **Proof-66 nickel three-cent pieces, Shield nickels, and Liberty Head nickels.**

   Nickel coins never have enjoyed the same kind of respect as their gold and silver cousins, but often they're rarer—and should be more valuable—in very high grades and with very sharp strikes. Being a harder metal, nickel doesn't yield crisp design details as readily as gold and silver when struck. And nickel coins are more prone to environmental damage over long periods of time, so fewer survive in pristine levels of preservation.

   Surviving populations of nineteenth-century nickel

coins are quite small in Proof-66, and at the height of the coin market's boom in 1989 some of these coins were bringing many thousands of dollars. Today, those same coins change hands for a great deal less. A coin that sold at auction for $8,000 in 1989 might well be available now for less than $1,000. And it's still every bit as rare.

Caution: Even though they may have been certified by one of the leading grading services, Proof-66 three-cent nickels, Shield nickels, and Liberty Head nickels should be free of carbon spots—that is, intense toning areas which appear to be black. If a coin has any of these spots, you should reject it, no matter how high the grade at which it has been certified.

8. **Capped Bust half dimes.**

The term "half dime" sounds strange to us today, since we're so accustomed to calling our five-cent piece the "nickel." In reality, however, the nickel as we know it is a relatively recent innovation. The five-cent piece wasn't introduced in its present size and composition until 1866. Up to then, and even after that for a few additional years, Americans used a small silver coin called the half dime.

Half dimes were among the earliest U.S. coins, making their first appearance in 1792. One of the earliest types was a coin known as the Capped Bust half dime, which showed Miss Liberty wearing an old-style cap. Half dimes of this type are very, very popular and also quite rare in top condition.

In Proof-66, Capped Bust half dimes are an exceptional value. They're far from inexpensive: At present, the sight-unseen price is about $30,000.

But that's not much more than the comparable price for a Proof-65 example, which currently is worth $25,000.

To get a really nice Proof-66 Capped Bust half dime, you're going to have to pay at least $35,000 or $36,000. But even that doesn't represent much of a premium over the Proof-65 price. If you have the choice of buying a Proof-65 or a Proof-66, you certainly should go for the 66.

These coins demonstrate that something can be a really terrific value even if it carries a hefty price tag.

9. **Franklin half dollars graded Proof-66 or Mint State-66 or higher.**

For several years, knowledgeable coin market insiders, including some of the nation's leading dealers, have been quietly acquiring superbly toned Franklin half dollars in very high grades—Proof-66 or Mint State-66 and above.

You would think that if you went to a coin show and walked from table to table trying to find nice Franklin halves, they'd be plentiful. These are, after all, modern coins—coins produced as recently as 1963. And their mintage levels certainly weren't small, by comparison with previous U.S. half dollars. Judging from their modest values in some of the price guides, you'd probably figure you ought to be able to find hundreds of these coins—maybe even buy them by the bag. You might expect to go up to Harry J. Forman, a highly regarded Philadelphia dealer who specializes in late-date U.S. coins, ask him for a roll of 1950 Franklin halves in Mint State-66, and have him produce not only a roll of 20 coins but a bag of 100 rolls.

This is one case, however, where even Harry Forman wouldn't be able to help you—for despite their seemingly plentiful mintage figures and despite what any price guides may say, high-grade Franklin halves are surprisingly scarce. And they're just not available in quantity.

It's true that the prices are modest. At this writing, a 1950 Franklin half dollar graded Mint State-66 by an independent grading service is priced at only about $125 sight-unseen. The problem is, hardly any 1950 halves are available in Mint State-66—at this price or even a higher price.

While insider dealers are aware of this situation and are seeking to benefit from it, collectors and investors as a whole haven't yet caught on. Thus, while the supply is low, the demand so far has also been relatively low. That has served to hold down the prices, at least on paper. Once additional people start looking for these coins and trying to obtain them, I look for the prices to rise dramatically. And since the present levels are so affordable, making these coins potentially attractive to such a broad spectrum of buyers, the price increase could be amazingly sharp.

I wouldn't be surprised to see high-grade Franklin halves that currently sell for $100 apiece soar in value to $300 each within a relatively short time. I wouldn't be at all surprised to see those 1950 halves in Mint State-66, now worth $125, skyrocket to the $500 to $1,000 range within the next ten years.

I don't expect this type of huge price increase to happen in the short term—within the next two years; I see it coming a little bit farther down the road. Therefore, if quick profit is your goal, you're probably better off buying something else. But if you can wait ten years, or even fifteen or twenty years, this is a great growth area.

10. Draped Bust dollars.

Silver dollars hold powerful appeal for investors. They're big, attractive coins with precious-metal content—assets that are quintessentially tangible. Early silver dollars, those produced in the nation's formative years, provide the added bonus of great rarity. Many of these coins had very low mintages, and the number of surviving examples is exceedingly small, especially in very high grades. Some are all but unknown even in the lowest Mint State levels.

Most of the very earliest U.S. silver dollars belong to a group known as the Draped Bust type. These coins bear a right-facing bust portrait of Miss Liberty with a garment draped over her shoulder, hence the name. The most famous of all U.S. silver dollars, the 1804, belongs to this group. Only fifteen specimens of this highly publicized rarity are known to exist, and all are accounted for as of this writing. One of them was sold at public auction in 1989 for $990,000, the highest price ever paid at auction up to that time for a single coin.

Unless you're a person of very substantial wealth, you probably can't expect to ever become the owner of an 1804 silver dollar. But the other Draped Bust dollars, from 1795 to 1803, are also highly desirable—and those can be obtained for significantly less than their world-renowned 1804 cousin.

None of these coins is cheap; all carry six-figure price tags in Mint State grades. But all have great potential to move up in value—perhaps to the seven-figure range—within the coming years as more and more institutional money enters the coin market. This is the type of coin that holds the greatest appeal for affluent members of the baby-boom generation, and the type that institutional investors will be seeking and acquiring with the greatest dedication.

Draped Bust dollars come with two different designs on the reverse. On the earliest examples, from 1795 to 1798, the reverse depicts a small eagle. In Mint State-67, one of these coins would cost more than $300,000 at the present time. From 1798 to the end of the series in 1804, the reverse portrayed a heraldic eagle.

The heraldic-eagle dollars from 1798 to 1803 strike me as particularly good investments at this time. The sight-unseen price is just $165,000 for a piece certified as Mint State-67 by one of the leading independent grading services, and you could probably get a super premium-quality specimen for not much more than $200,000. These are coins that may very well be trading for close to a million dollars a few years from now. Again, let me stress that you should buy only coins that are certified in these grades by one of the leading independent grading services.

These are very definitely not pocket-change rarities; they're about as far removed from that as anything in all of U.S. coinage. But they're coins that every collector dreams about owning someday—and coins that are dreams-come-true for a fortunate few.

Draped Bust dollars are exceedingly scarce even in the higher circulated grades. But specimens in Extremely Fine and Very Fine condition are findable treasures; Bust dollars in these grades are much more likely to turn up in your attic or cookie jar than a pristine Mint State example. You probably won't discover a Mint State piece unless it was purchased by someone in your family over the years.

If you do come across a Draped Bust dollar, don't sell it. These are coins with enormous investment potential and you should keep them.

Warning: The rare coin marketplace can be volatile. As this is written, all ten coins described in this chapter are excellent values. However, rapid changes in the marketplace could alter that situation; any or all of these coins may very well have experienced dramatic price increases (or decreases) by the time you read this. For that reason, you should check their prices carefully before making a purchase, and compare them to the prices listed here. In fact, you should do this before buying coins of any kind.

If any of these coins are selling for prices substantially higher than those listed here, use caution in considering their purchase. They may have already enjoyed the appreciation anticipated in this chapter, and thus may no longer be "sleepers." In that case, they will be removed from this special list in future editions of this book.

CHAPTER 11

COINS AND PRECIOUS METALS

Tangible assets.

Those two words express an entire world of financial commitment by investors.

In the late 1970s and early 1980s, the United States was wracked by a devastating combination of rampant inflation and high interest rates. Understandably nervous about the nation's economy, a great many Americans shifted large portions of their financial resources from conventional investments such as stocks, bonds, and real estate into tangible assets—things they could see, hold, and touch.

Rare coins became the focus of unprecedented public demand. People who had never collected coins poured millions and millions of dollars into the rare coin marketplace. They did this not because they wanted rare coins *per se*, but because in a sense coins were an offshoot of the single most coveted tangible asset of all: gold. Silver was also in great demand during that period, but gold was really the centerpiece of this massive investment move to tangible assets. People were buying gold almost by the truckload, driving the price of the timeless yellow metal to an all-time high of $887.50 an ounce on Jan. 21, 1980 (intra-day London high).

Gold is a universally recognized store of value. It's rare, aesthetically appealing, and remarkably resistant to corrosion. For all these reasons, it has long been used as a medium of exchange in many countries. In fact, the monetary system of the United States was originally based upon gold.

It has often been said that the value of gold doesn't change; what changes is how much everything else is worth in relation to gold. Thus, when gold rises in price from $350 to $400, what's really changing is the value of the dollar, not the value of the gold.

Gold is a mirror of the economic and political environment. When economics and politics are stable, the price of gold is relatively stable; in such a climate, in fact, the price of gold might even decline somewhat. But in times of economic and political instability, when the money supply is inflating, gold tends to increase in price—sometimes remarkably so.

During the turbulent period of the late 1970s and early 1980s, many analysts issued dramatic proclamations boldly predicting that gold would rise in price to levels never attained and hardly imagined before. Some foresaw a time when the price would soar as high as thousands of dollars per ounce.

These predictions haven't come true—at least so far. As this book is written, the price of gold is hovering around $400 an ounce. But even now, many financial advisors are flashing the buy signal for gold, arguing with conviction that its price will reach one, two, or three thousand dollars an ounce before the year 2000.

THE HARD-MONEY MOVEMENT

For many years, a dedicated group of financial advisors has been urging people to divert substantial portions of their money from bank accounts and other traditional savings repositories into tangible assets such as gold, silver, and numismatic (that is, collectible) coins. Well-known authors such as Howard Ruff, James Dines, and John P. Dessauer have been quoted widely as advocating the acquisition of "core holdings" containing these "hard" assets.

Sure, these experts say, you might want to invest in the stock market. Sure, you might want to put some of your money into bank accounts and into other traditional investment vehicles. But the possibility exists—and it's more than just a remote one—that this nation and indeed the entire world could face turbulent economic and political times in the months and years ahead, and at least a percentage of your holdings should be invested, as an insurance policy, in gold or silver or both.

Leaders of the hard-money, tangible-asset movement really do make a persuasive case. It certainly is possible that we could see instability in the world. Despite the easing of tensions and apparent dawn of democracy in Eastern Europe, trouble spots remain in a number of other locations. This became apparent in August 1990 when Iraq invaded Kuwait, precipitating a crude-oil crisis and heightening concern around the globe.

A protracted oil crisis could push up the price of gold significantly. An economic debacle such as the savings-and-loan crisis of the 1980s could prompt the United States government to print a lot more money, and that could cause massive inflation—yet another scenario that probably would cause gold and silver to soar in value.

There is, by the way, a widespread misconception that inflation means nothing more than higher prices. Actually, inflation means expansion of the money supply; in an inflated economy, there's more paper money around but each individual note is worth less.

Those who preach the gospel of acquiring tangible assets were scornful when government officials minimized the problems of the S&Ls and their impact on Americans' pocketbooks. They're similarly contemptuous when economic optimists tell us inflation is licked and won't be resurfacing soon. These "hard-money people" are sometimes accused of being doomsayers. Clearly, though, some of their critics are looking at events through rose-colored crystal balls.

Don't get the wrong impression about hard-money advocates. These people are very much like you and me. They invest part of their money, much of the time at least, in standard investment vehicles. More so than most of us, though, they believe in "hazard insurance" for their portfolios. They're acutely aware of the very real risks that exist in the world, and they're firmly convinced of the need to prepare financially for the worst. Gold, silver, and other tangible assets provide this kind of insurance, they believe.

People who purchase hard assets tend to cherish their privacy; they don't want the government knowing what they're buying and what they're keeping. In the early 1980s, these people were dismayed when the U.S. government put into place strong regulations governing transactions involving gold bullion. Under these regulations, buyers and sellers of gold bullion items must have their dealings reported to the Internal Revenue Service.

At that point, many of these people turned to rare coins, since these were not—and are not currently—subject to the same IRS reporting requirements. Rare coins are a relatively private investment.

Although the regulations dampened some buyers' enthusiasm for gold bullion, they haven't discouraged the leaders of the hard-money movement. These true believers remain as convinced as ever that the yellow metal's future is as bright as gold itself.

GOLD'S TWO PERSONALITIES

Gold and silver and other precious metals—but particularly gold—have what might be called two personalities. One of these is their long-term historical value; the other is their short-term price performance.

Gold has been aptly described as "financial insurance." John P. Dessauer, a noted financial advisor, has commented that gold is "better financial insurance than the FDIC will ever be." It has held its value for investors since the dawn of history, dating all the way back to the days of the pharaohs.

In the short term, however, gold can—and does—rise and fall in price quite unpredictably, and often very substantially. This is where some investors encounter difficulties: They focus too strongly on the short-term personality and lose sight of the metal's long-term aspect. They start out by purchasing gold as long-term insurance, but then get preoccupied with the profit motivation and try to make a killing on the metal. It's very important to keep the two goals separate.

Everybody should own at least a certain amount of gold as protection against the unexpected. Silver serves that function, too, and so does platinum. But gold has always enjoyed a primacy among the precious metals. Owning gold has been the way to preserve at least a minimum standard of living during times of political calamity. It has also been the best way—and sometimes the only way—to obtain safe passage out of a troubled land to a place where you can live in greater comfort and security. Gold was the ticket to freedom, for example, for thousands of Vietnamese refugees following the fall of Saigon in 1975.

How much gold should you own? That's like asking how much life insurance you should own. And the answer is much the same: You should own all the gold you can comfortably afford.

BULLION COINS

Bullion coins provide a convenient way to own precious metals—including not only gold but also silver and platinum. Although it is made in the form of a coin and carries a statement of value, a bullion coin is meant to be saved, rather than spent. It's intended to serve as a pocket-size investment, not a unit of commerce.

You can spend a bullion coin, but you'd lose a lot of money if you did, since the face value of such coins—the denomination placed on them by the government—is usually far lower than the value of the metal itself. The one-ounce gold American Eagle, for example, carries a face value of only $50, but the coin could be worth $400 or more as a piece of gold, and would cost that much to purchase.

Numismatic coins—rare coins—rise and fall in price in accordance with collector demand. Their value is determined by how scarce or common they are, and truly rare collector coins often sell for tens, hundreds, or even thousands of times their intrinsic worth. Bullion coins, by contrast, rise and fall directly in proportion to the value of the metal they contain. A one-ounce gold bullion coin, for example, would typically be priced just a little higher than the current market price of an ounce of gold. This small premium—generally less than 10 percent—covers such costs as production, distribution, and promotion.

As this is written, investors have their choice of a number of different gold, silver, and platinum bullion coins. In gold, they can choose from among such popular items as the American Eagle, the Canadian Maple Leaf, and the British Britannia. The American Eagle and Maple Leaf both have silver counterparts. And the Maple Leaf is made in platinum, too.

Bullion coins offer several attractive features. They're affordable, highly portable, easy to store, and readily salable. And the fact that they are coins—with legal-tender status in the country where they were issued—greatly enhances their liquidity.

Numismatic coins—precious-metal and otherwise—are sensitive not only to changes in demand among collectors but also to changes in global wealth. Their value tends to rise and fall in concert with personal income around the world. They have benefited, for instance, from the great wealth created in Japan. These coins are in demand from people who want them, like them, intend to keep them, and can afford to pay for them. At times when the world is reasonably sound economically and there's healthy economic growth, the likelihood is strong that numismatic coins will continue to appreciate in value.

WHAT'S IN STORE FOR PRECIOUS METALS?

It's safe and easy to say that precious metals—particularly gold—will rise in price substantially in a time frame of fifty or sixty years. Historically, the long-term trends have almost always been higher. It's far more difficult to say with any accuracy where the metals will be fifty days or fifty weeks from now. In the short term, their prices can be skewed enormously by an almost endless number of sometimes unforeseeable world events.

The difficulty of making such predictions was underscored during the 1980s. Some highly astute market analysts came out with forecasts that gold would soar well over $1,000—and even over $2,000—before the decade's end. Instead, the yellow metal languished around $400 as the Eighties drew to a close.

What will gold do in the next decade? Undaunted by the metal's lackluster performance in the Eighties, and their own recent misjudgments as prognosticators, experts remain optimistic. John Dessauer, for one, looks for gold to be trading for "$750 or even higher" by the year 2000 just in the normal course of market events. The price will go a great deal higher than that, he predicts, if some kind of economic or political catastrophe befalls the world or the nation.

If Dessauer is correct, the coming years will offer some golden opportunities to make big money buying gold and other precious metals. To do so, however, you'll need to adopt and maintain a longer-range perspective. The trick will be to buy when the price is right and then hold the metal—through short-term ups and downs—for several years. The chances are good that by the end of the decade, prices will be much higher and you'll then be able to sell for a tidy gain.

THE ORIGINAL GOLD BUG

James Dines is regarded as one of the founding fathers of the hard-money-asset movement. More than thirty years ago, as a securities analyst for A. M. Kidder and Company, Dines recommended the purchase of gold mining stocks to the firm's clients. Those recommendations panned out extremely well, and admirers have referred to Dines ever since as the original gold bug. This highly respected expert has published *The Dines Letter* for more than thirty years. His advice is eagerly sought on a personal level, as well—and it doesn't come cheap. Dines charges $10,000 for a speech and $5,000 an hour for private consultations.

One of Dines' most memorable—and spectacular—predictions came about 1970, when gold was valued at $35 an ounce and the Dow-Jones Industrial Average was hovering around 600. *The Dines Letter* predicted that these two numbers would cross one day—an almost unimaginable occurrence which actually did take place in January 1980. *Barron's*, the influential financial newspaper, described this in an editorial as one of the most fantastic investment calls ever made.

A few years ago, Dines made the same prediction again, and it seems just as daring this time as it did before. On July 19, 1990, with gold at $361 and the Dow-Jones Industrial Average close to 3,000, he predicted that these numbers would cross yet again. Later, he said this would happen during the 1990s.

Dines made this startling prediction in an interview which appeared in *The Rosen Numismatic Advisory*, an award-winning newsletter published by distinguished coin market analyst Maurice Rosen. Following is an excerpt from that interview. (Copyright 1990, *The Rosen Numismatic Advisory,* P.O. Box 38, Plainview, NY 11803, subscription price $79 per year.)

We've seemed to accustom ourselves to an inflation rate of 4–5% without worry or harm. What will cause inflation to soar and what level might it reach?

We are in a situation where matters are hopelessly out of control. Take the budget deficits which exist in the form of two "sets of books," one which shows us merely in a terrible fix, the other in a crisis situation. Look at the Saving & Loan crisis which started off as a "cost" in the $10–20 billion area—now up to $500 billion and counting! When you consider that the entire Money Stock (M-1) is about $810 billion you can see how enormous the problem really is. But that's just the first shoe; next are the banks which are in a worse situation because they are so thinly capitalized, with tons of bad loans and overpriced assets.

To bail out the S&Ls and the banks will cause massive amounts of money creation which in turn will cause inflation to skyrocket. Much higher inflation rates are virtually guaranteed, as are soaring prices for the whole inflation hedge sector. So, although your coin market is calm now, it will be performing superbly at some point in the future.

In 1980 the national debt was $1 trillion; now it's $3 trillion. The budget deficits continue apace, the banking situation disintegrates, our trade balance worsens, and on and on, yet the system is holding while gold is struggling. Why worry?

The Inflation Bubble is taking us through stages. The deflation of 1980–87 allowed further growth and expansion. Inflation asset values got too ahead of themselves in the '70s and corrected in the '80s. Since about 1982, gold has been in a broad trading range between 300 and 500. It's still way above 35. This is a huge base building area as we still digest the deflationary influences of the 1980–87 era—the biblical seven-year period of hard times. I see an increasing trend of inflation into the mid-1990s. What the peak rate will be hinges in what the politicians do. If they will continue to be as stupid as they have been we might get frightening high levels. If not, I can see 15–30% inflation.

Referring to the June 25, 1990, Wall Street Journal *article on gold, how did you arrive at your predictions of $2,000 and of $3,000–$5,000 gold prices?*

It's actually a compromise. If you want to bring the buying power of gold to where it was in 1934 before all this started you can come up with even substantially higher objectives. Old-time newsletter editor Vern Myers once told me $50,000 gold would be needed to put things back into balance. But, I feel $2,000–$5,000 would monetize gold enough so we could get back to a system that worked and we could tie down a lot of the remaining debt. Another way to look at it is by technical analysis using Fibonacci numbers, a method which has proven itself eerily accurate several times in the past. Since the 1980 high was $875, a Fibonacci multiple of 3 equals $2,665 and a multiple of 5 equals $4,375. Allowing for the sure-to-come panic at the end of this bullish gold move, $3,000–$5,000 is entirely possible.

Furthermore, the collapse of communism—something I've been predicting as far back as 1980—will be enormously bullish for gold as pent-up demand by ex-communist masses is unleashed. It all seems to be coming to a head later this decade; that's why I predict gold is at an absolutely bargain price today.

Besides the actual metal, I also recommend gold mining shares. I see them as being the absolutely best performing group over the next few years. Here, geographical diversification is important, which would-include North American, Australian, and South African issues. As the price of gold gets closer and closer to the Dow, just imagine the panic scramble that would result as individual stock investors and the big institutions buy into the relatively small gold-mining share industry. I'm sure you'll experience the same mad scramble of money coming into the rare coin market.

What advice do you have for rare coin investors in the years ahead?

I am adamantly against short-term trading. You should only buy for the long term. Like real estate, there's no more to be made and there are more collectors every year. There's huge pent-up demand, from China, Europe, and Russia to India and Africa. All of them will be competing for coins. You'll have more liquidity and greater acceptance from funds and banks. They are portable, beautiful works of art. The grading services have increased confidence and lowered spreads between buyer and seller.

Buyers of certain rare coins should not be overly concerned with price, as the opportunity to buy them does not come around often; buy them and lock them away. This is a good time to grab them as others get discouraged. This is like the early 1960s to me all over again. Of course, high inflation will send rare coin prices to the moon, and current psychology is all in favor of the smart investor buying now.

PRECIOUS METALS AND RARE COINS: SIMILARITIES AND DIFFERENCES

Bullion coins contain a relatively high amount of precious metal. Rare coins often contain little or none. Bullion coins' value comes from the metal itself. These coins are purely an investment in precious metal. Rare coins derive their value from collector demand—and this demand, in turn, stems from such factors as the coins' design and date. Rare coins can be partly a bullion investment, but they're mainly an investment in collector taste.

With bullion coins, the margin is very small between a dealer's bid and ask prices; with rare coins, the margin is much higher. The margin is the spread between what a dealer will pay for a coin and what he'll sell it for. With bullion coins, this spread may be only 3 or 4 percent, and sometimes even less. With rare coins, a spread of 15 or 20 percent is quite routine.

Bullion coins are standardized, and it isn't important to grade them; rare coins aren't standardized, and subtle differences between two similar coins can translate into a major variation in value. With bullion coins, you can buy ten, fifteen, or twenty pieces and they'll all be the same; you won't need a magnifying glass to inspect them. That's not true with rare coins. Even if a rare coin comes in a holder from a leading grading service, with an insert tab indicating its grade, that doesn't mean the coin is exactly the same as another coin in the same kind of holder with the same grade written on its tab. It also doesn't mean that the coin won't be graded differently if it is submitted again to the same service.

Bullion and bullion coins are subject to government regulation, but at present collector coins are not. Any time a person buys or sells bullion coins, the dealer has to fill out a Form 1099-B naming that person. A person buying or selling collector coins is entering into a relatively private transaction, as this book is written.

Bullion prices move up or down over a longer period; collector coins experience dramatic price changes almost instantaneously. In recent years, bullion has traded within a rather narrow price range, moving up or down only 10 or 15 percent even over a fairly extended period. Rare coins normally trade within a 5- to 15-percent price range, but it isn't uncommon for them to rise or fall as much as 20 to 50 percent in a short period. Volatility has been much more of a factor in the rare coin market than with bullion.

Bullion enjoys a much wider market than rare coins; the rare coin market is composed of thinly capitalized entrepreneurs. The market for gold is global and ranks among the world's most fully developed. It's also the most liquid of all the commodity markets. The rare coin marketplace is dramatically smaller. A few big investment firms tested the waters—Kidder, Peabody and Merrill Lynch, among them. But at this writing, the rare coin industry doesn't yet enjoy the full participation of companies such as this.

COIN AND PRECIOUS METAL PRICES

Does a correlation exist between the prices of precious metals and those of rare coins? There has been considerable discussion and analysis regarding this possibility. After all, both of these assets are in a sense indicators of where wealthy people think the economy and political events are headed.

In a "micro-sense," as economists would refer to it, there isn't really a day-to-day correlation. If a rare coin is valued at $10,000 and gold goes from $360 to $375 an ounce, the value of that coin isn't going to change. However, in a broader sense, or "macro-sense," as economists would call it, a correlation does exist in the long run.

In the early 1970s, gold was extremely strong and so were rare coins. From 1974 to the early part of 1977, gold was in the doldrums and so were rare coins. Then, from 1977 to 1980, rare coins and gold both did extremely well.

Take a look at the accompanying chart entitled "Does Spot Gold Matter?" In it, you'll see the "spot" price of gold—the market price of one troy ounce of the metal—traced from January of 1985 to June of 1990, along with the corresponding prices for common-date Saint-Gaudens double eagles and Liberty Head double eagles ($20 gold pieces).

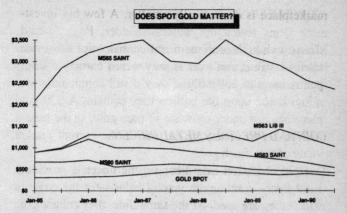

Graph of gold bullion and "semi-numismatic" coin price performance. (Graph courtesy Coin Dealer Newsletter)

In this chart, Saint-Gaudens double eagles graded Mint State-60 and Mint State-63 correlate somewhat with the spot price of gold. So do Mint State-63 Liberty Type 3 double eagles. But Mint State-65 Saint-Gaudens double eagles, which are really collector coins, show very little direct correlation. At one point, these coins were actually decreasing in value at a time when gold was increasing.

We can conclude from this chart that the price of gold is an important psychological factor in the rare coin marketplace, but it doesn't necessarily stimulate gold coins to rise or fall in value. It does affect the value of what we would call "semi-bullion" numismatic coins—coins like Mint State-60 Saint-Gaudens double eagles. But its impact is less direct, and may even be negligible, on higher-grade coins that are pure collectibles.

CONCLUSIONS

Coins with high precious-metal content have substantial intrinsic value, and even if they weren't worth a single penny more as collectibles, they'd still command a premium based upon the bullion they contain. A $20 gold piece has just under an ounce of pure gold, so the least it will be worth at any given time is the current market value of that much gold.

Gold and silver and other precious metals provide a solid floor—a minimum market value—for the coins in which they are used. At the same time, they enhance the appearance and appeal of these coins, and this gives them greater allure as collectibles.

The price of a numismatic coin is a product of supply and demand, and gold and silver content can influence this equation by increasing the level of demand. A rare coin can be worth many thousands of dollars without containing a bit of precious metal; many cents and nickels bring very fancy prices. But, in practical terms, a great many buyers have shown a decided preference for coins that contain gold or silver.

The impact of precious metal is far more direct in "bullion" coins. The value of these coins at any particular moment is directly linked to the price of the precious metal from which they're made. If the price of gold or silver goes up or down even marginally, the prices of bullion coins will do likewise.

Bullion coins essentially are economic hedges—a convenient form of insurance against inflation. Numismatic coins are collectibles, but their long-term price performance has given them the dimension of good investments as well.

CHAPTER 12

COIN DEALERS, DRUG DEALERS, AND THE GOVERNMENT

Because they combine great value with small size and easy portability, rare coins hold special appeal for people who want to keep their wealth concealed and be able to move it around.

Most of the time, these people's motivations are perfectly legitimate; they're reputable investors who wish to maintain low profiles. But the very same attributes that make coins attractive to legitimate investors and collectors have also caught the eye of profit-minded people on the wrong side of the law.

*982 gold coins valued over $2 million, all buried treasure of drug
dealers. It was all sold at public auction at the direction of the
U.S. government. (Photo courtesy Heritage Capital Corp.)*

This is not a strictly modern-day phenomenon. Centuries
ago, pirates hoarded coins in chests of buried treasure. In
recent years, however, space-age criminals have found
an updated way to use rare coins—and bullion coins,
too—to their advantage.

One of the most intriguing examples of this came to
light in 1988, when Heritage Numismatic Auctions Inc.
of Dallas, one of the nation's largest and best-known coin
auction companies, held a public sale featuring valuable
gold coins that federal agents had confiscated from members of an international drug ring.

The drug dealers had purchased large numbers of coins—
rare coins and bullion coins, as well—to help conceal the
proceeds from their illicit activities. And I do mean *conceal*: They had transformed some of the coins, quite liter-

ally, into modern-day buried treasure by hiding them in underground caches.

To put the story in proper perspective, we have to go back two years earlier, when members of the drug ring were arrested on a variety of drug, racketeering, and tax-evasion charges. Hoping to obtain lighter sentences, they agreed to a plea bargain—and part of that agreement called for them to forfeit their coins.

Finding these coins wasn't a simple matter of going to one of the suspects' safety deposit box. The coins were hidden in three separate locations: buried in plastic bags beneath a Nebraska field, in a briefcase under a rockpile in the Colorado Rockies, and stashed on the Hawaiian island of Maui.

"It was very much like treasure hunting," said Thomas J. Dolan, one of the agents who coordinated the investigation for the federal Drug Enforcement Administration. "Part of it was out in the guy's back yard, and we went in with a bulldozer and a map."

One of the conspirators had drawn up a crude map showing the location of one hoard of gold coins buried by the ring in the small town of Crawford, Nebraska—population 1,320. The map said the coins could be found between two pine trees seventeen paces apart, and it showed a "white cliff with a crack" as a point of reference.

The ground was frozen the day DEA agents went to retrieve the treasure, so they brought in a backhoe to help with the excavation. They found the coins just where the map said they would be—sealed inside Tupperware containers.

A second cache of coins was buried elsewhere on the property, but this one proved easier to unearth. A hole had already been dug at this site, then covered with a 2×10 board and mounds of earth.

In Colorado, the conspirators apparently ran out of Tupperware. This time, the coins were found in a brief-case that was wedged in a rocky crevasse. The DEA had no trouble determining the owner: The briefcase was tagged with a United Airlines baggage claim check.

One of the leaders of the drug cartel apparently had some knowledge of the coin market, for the treasure included a number of unusually rare and desirable items. Among the highlights:

- A virtually complete set of Liberty Head double eagles ($20 gold pieces).
- An almost complete set of Saint-Gaudens eagles ($10 gold pieces).
- Dozens of early $10 gold pieces.
- Two high-relief 1907 double eagles.
- An 1879 stella (or $4 gold piece), a rare pattern coin worth tens of thousands of dollars.

The bullion portion of the cache contained nearly $1 million worth of bullion-type gold coins and bars, including 1,132 Canadian Maple Leafs, 399 South African Kruger-rands, 303 Russian Chervonets, and two 100-ounce bars. Heritage sold these items privately for the government.

Heritage sold the numismatic material at two auctions in October and December 1988, where the coins brought approximately $2 million—well above presale expectations. This money was placed in the U.S. Treasury's general fund.

The drug ring involved in this case operated out of Denver, but had "tentacles" in San Diego and South America, according to the DEA.

Tom Dolan, who is group supervisor of the DEA

office in Denver, said the drug dealers purchased the coins and bullion "as one of the ploys they used" to hide their ill-gotten gains. They also spent large sums of drug-related money to acquire other items such as real estate and stocks.

The Comprehensive Crime Control Act of 1984 empowers the DEA and other federal agencies to confiscate and sell any items which they believe were purchased with the proceeds of illegal activities, such as drug trafficking and racketeering. Often, the proceeds from such sales are shared on a pro-rata basis with state and local law-enforcement agencies who assist in making the arrests and seizures.

According to the DEA, the Heritage auction represented the largest public sale of confiscated collectibles ever arranged by the agency. Most of the coins were high-grade circulated specimens. However, there were also a number of proof and Mint State pieces. This was not the first time coins seized by the government had been sold on the public's behalf; however, it was easily the biggest such sale ever held.

Among the other collectibles confiscated and sold in recent years were a group of Tiffany lamps and a 1963 Ferrari GTO automobile. The car was sold privately for $1.6 million, according to Steve Boyle, a spokesman for the U.S. Marshal Service, which arranges most such sales.

CASH AND YOUR COIN PURCHASES

The U.S. Treasury Department has promulgated a new regulation which—while apparently aimed in part at identifying drug dealers—could also have implications for coin dealers and their customers.

For years, there has been a federal rule requiring that the Internal Revenue Service must be notified of any cash transaction of $10,000 or more. But the Treasury broadened this on July 24, 1990, to require the reporting of "related" cash transactions over a twelve-month period which, in their aggregate, total $10,000 or more. This rule was made retroactive to Dec. 31, 1989.

For those who are anxious to preserve their financial privacy, this rule poses serious potential problems.

EPILOGUE

Rare coins provide rare opportunities. Although they are only pocket-size, they possess enormous attractions: historical significance ... beautiful art ... high value ... great collector appeal ... and, in some instances, investment potential.

One-Minute Coin Expert has given you all the knowledge you need to harness these assets and make them work for you.

I've shown you how to find a fortune in your pocket change—how to sift through the ordinary coins in your pocket and purse and discover the extraordinary coins that lie hidden there, totally overlooked by most people.

I've shown you what to look for in that long-forgotten cigar box in your attic, or that cookie jar filled with coins on a kitchen shelf—how to identify coins that are worth a small fortune among these seemingly humble family hoards.

Venturing into the far-flung coin marketplace, where rare coins are bought and sold by thousands of entrepreneurs, I've given you vital insights into how to measure the market's current mood—how to size up its psychology—and how to make this knowledge work to your advantage. I've stressed the importance of not simply following the crowd. Remember this advice: When everyone seems to be buying, you should be selling, and when everyone seems to be selling, you should be buying.

I've told you how coins are graded, and how a coin's grade directly affects its market value. I've demonstrated why an improperly graded coin could be just as devastating to you financially as one that is overpriced.

I've shown you how coins can be traded very much like stocks—coins that have been independently certified by grading services such as the Professional Coin Grading Service, the Numismatic Guaranty Corporation, and ANACS.

I've told you how you can make big profits from small coins and shown you how to cash in those profits. I've even supplied a secret list of ten "sleeper" coins—coins with high potential to increase in value dramatically.

I've explained how rare coins are related to precious metals, and discussed both the similarities and the differences between rare coins and "bullion" coins. And I've shown how even drug dealers find rare coins and bullion highly appealing.

Back in the 1970s, many investors didn't know how to deal with rampant inflation. The strategies they employed were unsophisticated and smacked of excessive trial and error. Today, the investment market is more mature—and rare coins have assumed an increasingly important role in many investors' plans and portfolios.

Some economic forecasters are predicting that inflation will return in coming years with a vengeance. If inflation does come raging back, rare coins would surely soar in value.

This time people would know how to protect themselves against the ravages of inflation, and that protection would certainly include massive purchases of gold and silver bullion as well as heavy emphasis on rare coins as time-proven hedges.

But many coins have excellent potential for appreciation in value—irrespective of inflation or any other economic variable.

Follow the blueprint in *One-Minute Coin Expert*, and you'll be prepared for any marketplace. You'll be ready and able to protect both yourself and your coins.

Reread the book, and enjoy it. Then use it like the expert you've become!

INVITATION FOR CORRESPONDENCE

The author welcomes reports of your pocket-change finds and your questions about coin investing at: Scott Travers Rare Coin Galleries, Inc., P. O. Box 1711, F.D.R. Station, New York, NY 10150. Telephone: 212/535-9135. E-mail: travers@inch.com

AMERICAN NUMISMATIC ASSOCIATION
MEMBERSHIP APPLICATION FORM

❏ **Yes,** I want to be a part of America's Coin Club. I understand that I will receive the Association's monthly magazine *The Numismatist*, access to 30,000 books in the world's largest Numismatic lending library, discounts on numismatic books and dozens of other exclusive member benefits.

Name_____

Address _____

C/S/Z _____

I herewith make application for membership in the American Numismatic Association, subject to the bylaws of the Association. I also agree to abide by the Code of Ethics adopted by the Association.

Signature _____

❏ **Enclosed is $35 for a 1 yr. membership**
To Join With a Credit Card Call
1-800-367-9723
Or Return Application to:
American Numismatic Association
818 N. Cascade Avenue
Colorado Springs, CO 80903-3279